Database Management
with dBase and SQL

CHAPMAN & HALL COMPUTING SERIES

Database Management with dBase and SQL

A practical introduction

Hans Pruyt

Erasmus University, The Netherlands

Translated by Mike Lewis

CHAPMAN & HALL

London · Glasgow · New York · Tokyo · Melbourne · Madras

Published by Chapman & Hall, 2–6 Boundary Row, London SE1 8HN

Chapman & Hall, 2–6 Boundary Row, London SE1 8HN, UK

Blackie Academic & Professional, Wester Cleddens Road, Bishopbriggs, Glasgow G64 2NZ, UK

Van Nostrand Reinhold Inc., 115 5th Avenue, New York NY10003, USA

Chapman & Hall Japan, Thomson Publishing Japan, Hirakawacho Nemoto Building, 6F, 1–7–11 Hirakawa-cho, Chiyoda-ku, Tokyo 102, Japan

Chapman & Hall Australia, Thomas Nelson Australia, 102 Dodds Street, South Melbourne, Victoria 3205, Australia

Chapman & Hall India, R. Seshadri, 32 Second Main Road, CIT East, Madras 600 035, India

First English language edition 1993

© 1993 Hans Pruyt

Original Dutch language edition – Gegevens en Relaties: Een praktische inleiding database management met dBase IV/SQL – 1989, Hans Pruyt.
Published by Samson Bedrijfs Informatie 6v.

Printed by TJ Press (Padstow) Ltd, Padstow, Cornwall

ISBN 0 412 47750 5

A catalogue record for this book is available from the British Library

Library of Congress Cataloging-in-Publication data available

∞ Printed on permanent acid-free text paper, manufactured in accordance with the proposed ANSI/NISO Z 39.48-199X and ANSI Z 39.48-1984

Contents

Contents

Contents

Contents

Preface

This book is aimed at readers who want to learn the essentials of database management without being distracted by peripheral details. It concentrates on practical work rather than the purely theoretical aspects. dBASE IV is a good platform for learning this subject, but only a few of its many commands and functions – and there are nearly five hundred of them – are vital for this. In this book, I have selected just those features which will allow you to master the essentials quickly. You will then be in a good position to expand your knowledge further in any direction you wish.

The book covers the following topics:

Introduction to database management
In the introductory chapters, the emphasis is on those aspects which are common to most database systems. The basic principles of design are also covered.

Practical information
The book gives the reader practical instructions for working with dBASE IV.

SQL
The book includes a fairly detailed overview of SQL, which is the standard language for database management. This part of the book will help the reader to acquire a full understanding of the language, especially if read at the same time as undertaking hands-on practice. Details are also given of the various ways of using interactive and menu-driven dBASE IV commands in conjunction with SQL.

Basic principles of programming
The basic concepts of programming are covered. Although they are described in the context of the dBASE programming language, they are in fact general principles which apply to virtually all programming languages.

Applications
By means of examples and accompanying explanations, the book

shows how to create simple – though certainly not trivial – applications using dBASE IV. This is achieved by combining SQL with the dBASE programming language. This part of the book goes deeper into the subject than the documentation supplied with dBASE IV itself.

Further topics
To round things off, the book touches on a number of additional topics which the reader will find useful. These include: advanced features of the dBASE language; import and export of data; presentation and further analysis of data; systems for more than one user; and client/server systems.

Summary of commands and functions
As well as the detailed material presented in the main part of the book, there is also a summary of all the commands and functions covered.

Who is the book intended for?
The book is primarily aimed at students in higher education. No previous knowledge of programming or mathematics is required. It is also suitable as material for self-study, a fact which can also make the teacher's job easier. In fact, the book is likely to appeal anyone who has access to a computer on which dBASE IV has been installed and who wishes to delve deeper into the subject of database management.

Database management is an excellent starting-point for any serious course on information technology, for three reasons. The first is the enormously important role which database management plays in modern information systems. Secondly, database management offers an excellent opportunity to learn another essential aspect of information technology: programming. It can do this in a much better way than by teaching 'pure' programming, for example with Pascal or C. Those languages take considerably longer to learn, and the people learning them often end up writing trivial 'toy' programs. On the other hand, genuinely useful applications can be developed rapidly by using just a subset of the dBASE language.

The third reason is that database management is a gratifying subject to teach. This is because it requires the student to develop genuine insights. By contrast, the teaching of some other computer applications consists of little more than telling the student which buttons to press.

Preface

dBASE IV/SQL is a suitable platform for learning database management because the knowledge which you will gain will not tie you to one particular software package or hardware environment. SQL is the undisputed industry-wide standard for database management systems, on workstations, minicomputers and mainframes. The dBASE language has for a long time ceased to be the exclusive property of the publishers of dBASE, and is now supported by many other software products. Examples of systems that use dialects of dBASE are FoxPro, Clipper and Arago. The name 'X-Base' has recently been proposed as a non-proprietary alternative to dBASE.

Measured by the number of applications which have been developed, X-Base is without doubt the most widely used language on PCs. Because X-Base is much easier to learn than the more traditional languages like Cobol, Pascal and C, it has brought about a certain democratisation of the application development process. X-Base has recently become available on minicomputers and UNIX workstations.

dBASE IV offers an elegant integration of X-Base and SQL. The arrival of client/server systems, in which a PC runs an X-Base application and uses SQL commands to share data with a 'back-end' database running on another machine, can only increase the importance of the package.

Acknowledgements

It is a pleasure for me to record my thanks to the many people who have helped me in the preparation of this book.

As soon as it became obvious that dBASE IV would not meet its planned release date, Mark de Visser of Ashton-Tate (now Borland) arranged for me to have a pre-release version. This made it possible for me to start preparing the book in good time. Marja Baas of Ashton-Tate kept me informed of all the developments concerning dBASE IV and was helpful in providing an evaluation copy. Wim Hoek of Borland put a copy of the dBASE IV Server Edition at my disposal.

Wil Bouwman, Carlo Cozzi, Kees Hellinga, Brigitte ter Horst, Hans Koetsenruijter, Jan Koster, Wim du Mortier, Gerry Nicolaas, Rob Pruyt, Désirée Schipper, Martin Sinnige, Ankie Smit, Willem Snapper, Marga Stegeman, Jaap Vink and Jacobien van den Voorden read the draft and offered comments. Luc Dorpmans and Marc Hovens Greve gave valuable technical advice.

I would also like to thank the students on the information

xi

technology courses at the Faculty of Social Sciences at Erasmus University, Rotterdam, who worked with the draft version of this text. Robert Anjie, as well as several other students, drew my attention to points in the Dutch text which needed correcting.

I am grateful to Dick Brinkman of the publishers Samsom Uitgeverij bv and to Mike Lewis for their help in bringing about an English language version of the book.

Finally, I would like to thank my academic colleagues who evaluated the Dutch text. Almost unanimously, they requested that I give more attention to the theoretical aspects of database management (a request which, for some inexplicable reason, I did not receive from a single student). I have tried to follow this suggestion – but not, I hope, at the expense of the relaxed character of the text.

Any remaining mistakes are entirely my own responsibility. I welcome further comments and suggestions from the readers of this book.

Hans Pruyt
Rotterdam, January 1992

Translator's preface

For this English version, I have tried to keep the relaxed yet authoritative style which is a characteristic of the original Dutch edition. I have not altered any of the program code, apart from substituting English-like variable names where necessary. In the sample Housing database, I have created entirely new data, using addresses, names of property companies and house prices which are likely to be more familiar to English-speaking readers. The basic design of the database, however, has not been altered.

Mike Lewis
Edinburgh, April 1992

CHAPTER ONE

Introduction

A **database** is an organised collection of data: a model of some aspect of the real world, stored inside a computer.

At one time, you would only find databases in large organisations such as big companies and government departments. But since the mid 1980s, databases have been springing up everywhere: from multi-national corporations to community organisations and voluntary groups. There is scarcely an area of life where databases have not made their mark.

Although most people think of databases in terms of business and management systems, they have many other uses. For example, databases have for a long time played a role in research in the social sciences. In his 1956 study *The Power Elite*, the sociologist C. Wright Mills used a file (of punched cards) to store information about the careers of US presidents, members of the cabinet, and members of the US Supreme Court.[1]

A **database management system** (DBMS for short) is a computer program which serves as a tool for storing data in a database, for retrieving information from it and for keeping it up to date. The rather loose term 'electronic card file' is sometimes used to describe a DBMS.

An important point about the DBMS is that it is a **general** tool for working with data; it is not limited to any particular application. This is in contrast to other types of data-handling programs, where the program is designed for a specific type of data, such as statistical data or stock control records. With a DBMS, the same program can be used with totally different information. In fact, DBMSs are suitable for anything from inventory records and survey results to shipping movements or details of archeological relics.

Storing, retrieving and updating data involves a complex series of actions on the part of the computer. The DBMS must be capable of

---

[1]Mills describes his methods of working in Mills (1959), p.232.

accepting a relatively simple instruction from the user – to find a particular item of data, for instance – and converting it into the actions which the computer must execute in order to perform the task as efficiently as possible.

The more sophisticated DBMSs are also **programmable**. This means that they allow people to create ready-made systems for other, less technical, people to use. These systems can include menus and data-entry forms which provide a user-friendly way of working with the database.

Most database management systems, including dBASE IV, are **relational**. Other types of DBMS exist, including hierarchical and network. However, these are used much less often.[1] The most important characteristic of the relational database is that it appears to the user as a collection of tables (in Appendix E, we will look at the workings of relational DBMS in more detail). The technical aspects of how the tables are stored is largely irrelevant to the user.[2]

---

[1]See Date (1990), Appendix B and C.

[2]Relational DBMSs are particularly suitable for storing structured data. An example of the sort of data they are less suitable for would be long passages of text. For two short articles on this point, see Pruyt (1991), Schipper (1991).

CHAPTER TWO

Database management: an overview

2.1 A sample database

The easiest way of understanding what database management is all about is to look at an example. Throughout this book, we will work with a sample database concerned with the residential housing market. Although the data in it is entirely fictitious, it does represent the type of application which you are likely to come across in real life.

The sample database contains objective information about residential properties. It includes facts about specific houses, as well as details of sales and purchases of houses – the sort of information which you are likely to find in land registry files[1]. Its aim is to assist with research into housing need and the activities of property companies in the housing sector. It might be used by researchers, journalists, local authority officials or pressure group workers.

The database holds, among other details, the following information about properties:

> Property number
> House number
> Street
> Year of construction
> Structural condition (P for poor, A for average, G for good)

Let's start by telling the DBMS simply to display the basic property data on the screen. To tell the DBMS to do something, you give **instructions**. In the case of dBASE IV/SQL, you would type two instructions. First:

```
START DATABASE Property;
```

---

[1]This does not apply in all countries.

to open the database; then:

```
SELECT *
FROM Property;
```

to display the required data on the screen. The data appears as a table:

PROPNUM	HOUSENUM	STREET	YEARC	CONDITN
1	121	Wellington St.	1899	A
2	123	Wellington St.	1899	A
3	119	Wellington St.	1899	A
4	117	Wellington St.	1899	A
5	115	Wellington St.	1899	P
6	113	Wellington St.	1898	P
7	111	Wellington St.	1898	P
8	109	Wellington St.	1898	P
9	120	Park Road	1898	P
10	122	Park Road	1898	G

The complete set of instructions available for use with the DBMS is known as a **query language**. Many different kinds of query language exist, but the best known is Structured Query Language, or SQL. SQL has developed into a standard which is recognised throughout the computer industry – despite the fact that different vendors insist on introducing minor differences in the versions which they supply.

SQL's role as an industry standard provides an important advantage for users. It means that they are not tied to a specific vendor. They can gain experience on one DBMS and then apply it to the systems produced by almost every other vendor. SQL achieved this distinction mainly because it was promoted by the largest computer manufacturer, IBM.

SQL is different from some other query languages in that it is **non-procedural**. This means that the user only has to specify **what** data he wants to extract from the database. He does not have to worry about **how** the data is stored or how to go about retrieving it.

An example of a **procedural** language is the traditional dBASE language. It is found both in dBASE III Plus and dBASE IV; in the latter it exists alongside SQL. Users of the dBASE language must usually specify the various steps needed to retrieve the data in more detail than they would with SQL.

Let's now look at some examples of how queries are constructed in

A sample database

SQL. The aim here is merely to give a flavour of what's possible. More detailed explanations will be given in later chapters.

In the previous example, we saw how to display **all** the data. You can, however, be more selective in choosing the data to retrieve. If you just wanted to see the house number and street name of each property, you would type:

```
SELECT HouseNum, Street
FROM Property;
```

The result would be:

HOUSENUM	STREET
121	Wellington St.
123	Wellington St.
119	Wellington St.
117	Wellington St.
115	Wellington St.
113	Wellington St.
111	Wellington St.
109	Wellington St.
120	Park Road
122	Park Road

Going further, you might want to identify those properties which are in poor condition:

```
SELECT *
FROM Properties
WHERE Conditn = 'P';
```

The results would appear as follows:

PROPNUM	HOUSENUM	STREET	YEARC	CONDITN
5	115	Wellington St.	1899	P
6	113	Wellington St.	1898	P
7	111	Wellington St.	1898	P
8	109	Wellington St.	1898	P
9	120	Park Road	1898	P

Or you could ask for all properties in poor condition that were built after 1898:

5

```
SELECT *
FROM Property
WHERE Conditn='P'
AND YearC > 1898;
```

which would give:

PROPNUM	HOUSENUM	STREET	YEARC	CONDITN
5	115	Wellington St.	1899	P

The data can also be updated. The following instruction retrieves all properties in Park Road and changes their condition to Good:

```
UPDATE Property
SET Conditn = 'G'
WHERE Street = 'Park Road';
```

The computer replies:

```
2 row(s) updated
```

Although SQL is called a **query** language, it can do a great deal more than answer questions. For example, it includes an instruction for creating new 'tables'. Our Property table was created with this instruction:

```
CREATE TABLE Property
(PropNum INTEGER, HouseNum CHAR(6), Street CHAR(20),
YearC SMALLINT, Conditn CHAR(1));
```

It can also add new records to the table. The following instruction was used to add the property at 121 Wellington Street to the table:

```
INSERT INTO Property
VALUES (1, '121', 'Wellington Street',1899, 'A'));
```

A single database can be made up of several different tables. As well as information about the properties themselves, our example database contains a table showing details of the sales of properties. This has the following items: the property number, the date of the sale, the price, the name of the buyer and the name of the seller.

A sample database

PROP-NUM	SALE-DATE	PRICE	BUYER	SELLER
1	25/02/80	25000	FX Properties Ltd	P Johnson
6	01/12/81	22500	Vista Estates Ltd	T Taylor
1	26/02/80	40000	Vista Estates Ltd	FX Properties Ltd
1	27/02/80	50000	Ballerton D.C.	Vista Estates Ltd
3	11/11/81	17500	Ballerton D.C.	T Zander
8	01/01/82	20000	Vista Estates Ltd	L Lauder
9	30/01/82	30000	Vista Estates Ltd	W Bendix
10	05/05/83	35000	FX Properties Ltd	I Stevenson
10	22/05/83	37500	Vista Estates Ltd	FX Properties Ltd

SQL makes it easy to combine information from the property table with the sales table. For example, we could find out which properties have been sold and at what price:

```
SELECT HouseNum, Street, Price
FROM Property, Sales
WHERE Property.PropNum = Sales.PropNum;
```

The result would be:

PROPERTY->HOUSENUM	PROPERTY->STREET	SALES->PRICE
121	Wellington St.	25000
121	Wellington St.	40000
121	Wellington St.	50000
119	Wellington St.	17500
113	Wellington St.	22500
109	Wellington St.	20000
120	Park Road	30000
122	Park Road	35000
122	Park Road	37500

For another example, the next query asks for properties which have been sold for more than £45,000.

```
SELECT HouseNum, Street
FROM Property
WHERE PropNum IN
    (SELECT PropNum
    FROM Sales
    WHERE Price > 45000);
```

7

The result is:

```
HOUSENUM   STREET
121        Wellington St.
```

In Chapter 6, we will look in more detail at queries involving data from more than one table.

2.2 Basic terminology

A **database** is a structured collection of **tables**. Each table has a **name**:

```
table: Country
COUNTRY     CAPITAL
England     London
Scotland    Edinburgh
Wales       Cardiff
```

Each table is concerned with one or other 'object' or person, in this case countries. This basic subject of the table is sometimes called its **entity**.

The table's column names are called **attributes**. In this example, Country and Capital are attributes. The term **field name** is often used as an alternative for attribute.

The table's rows are called **records**. (In academic usage, you might also come across the term **tuple**.)

```
England     London
```

is therefore one record. Records are equivalent to the individual cards in a card file.

Inside a record, there are **fields**. A field corresponds to a column in the table. So England and Scotland are each the contents of a field. Another word for field is **cell**, though this is less often used.

CHAPTER THREE

dBASE IV/SQL on your computer

This chapter contains practical information about using SQL within dBASE IV.

3.1 Starting dBASE IV

The first step is to start up the dBASE IV program. You do this with the Dos command:

```
DBASE
```

How dBASE IV appears when you start it up depends on how it was installed. If it was installed to start working with SQL straight away, you would see the **SQL prompt**[1] (see Fig. 3.1). This prompt means that the system is ready to accept SQL commands.

It is more likely that dBASE IV will start by displaying the **Control Centre** (see Fig. 3.2). This is a system of menus which gives access to many of dBASE IV's functions. However, it is not really relevant to SQL. To get rid of it, press the Escape key and, when dBASE asks for confirmation, reply by pressing Y.

On leaving the Control Centre, you should see a single dot at the bottom left corner of the screen. This is called the **dot prompt**. It indicates that dBASE is ready to accept commands. You should enter the following command:

```
SET SQL ON
```

After a moment, the following will appear:

```
SQL.
```

---

[1]Various installation settings are stored in a file named Config.Db. If this file contains the command SQL = ON, the SQL prompt will appear as soon as you start dBASE IV.

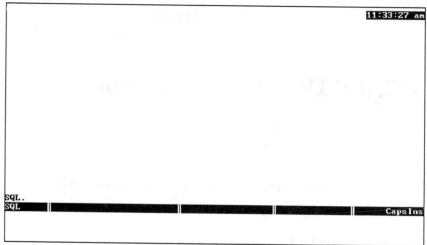

Fig. 3.1 Screen showing the SQL prompt.

This is also a prompt. It tells us that we can now enter SQL commands.

3.2 Opening an existing database

Before we can do anything with the data in a database, we must first **open** the database. To open an existing database – in this case our sample Housing database – type the following command:

```
START DATABASE Housing;
```

The system will open the database and make it ready for use.
To see the names of all existing databases, use this command:

```
SHOW DATABASE;
```

This displays a list of the names of all the databases available in the system.

Once a database has been opened, you can enter SQL commands for creating tables, searching for data, making selections, and so on.

3.3 Creating an empty database

If you do not yet have a database, you must start by creating a new one. Enter a command such as the following:

```
CREATE DATABASE MyData;
```

10

```
┌──────────────────────────────────────────────────────────────────────────┐
│ Catalog   Tools   Exit                                       ▐1:55:42 pm▌ │
│                          dBASE IV CONTROL CENTER                           │
│                    CATALOG: C:\DBASE\DATA\PROJECTS.CAT                      │
│                                                                            │
│    Data        Queries      Forms       Reports      Labels    Applications│
│  ┌─────────┐ ┌─────────┐ ┌─────────┐ ┌─────────┐ ┌─────────┐ ┌─────────┐  │
│  │<create> │ │<create> │ │<create> │ │<create> │ │<create> │ │<create> │  │
│  │         │ │         │ │         │ │         │ │         │ │         │  │
│  │ASSEMBLY │ │LOCATOR  │ │         │ │ALLNAMES │ │         │ │         │  │
│  │CLIENT   │ │NAMESQRY │ │         │ │CARDREC  │ │         │ │         │  │
│  │ITEMS    │ │         │ │         │ │REGIONAL │ │         │ │         │  │
│  │▐PEOPLE ▌│ │         │ │         │ │         │ │         │ │         │  │
│  │SALES    │ │         │ │         │ │         │ │         │ │         │  │
│  │         │ │         │ │         │ │         │ │         │ │         │  │
│  └─────────┘ └─────────┘ └─────────┘ └─────────┘ └─────────┘ └─────────┘  │
│                                                                            │
│  File:       ▐C:\DBASE\SAMPLES\PEOPLE.DBF▌                                 │
│  Description: ▐Everybody who took part in the survey▌                      │
│                                                                            │
│  Help:F1  Use:◀─┘  Data:F2  Design:Shift-F2  Quick Report:Shift-F9  Menus:F10│
└──────────────────────────────────────────────────────────────────────────┘
```

Fig. 3.2 The Control Centre.

This command creates an empty database called MyData. You may choose any name you like in place of MyData (to a maximum of eight characters).

3.4 Files and directories

dBASE IV/SQL itself keeps track of which databases are present in the system and where they are located. For most of the time, you do not need to be concerned with the files in which the databases are stored.

For each SQL database, dBASE IV creates a sub-directory[1]. The name of this sub-directory is the same as the name of the database. Suppose, for example, that you started dBASE from a directory named \TEST. If you then created a database called Housing,

─────────────────────

[1]You can think of the computer's disk as being divided into a number of sections, each of which is a separate sub-directory. Each sub-directory can hold further sub-directories, which can in turn hold still further sub-directories, and so on. Sub-directories therefore form a sort of 'tree structure'.

A sub-directory can also hold files. The full name of a particular file consists of the 'path' which must be taken through the tree structure in order to reach the file. For example, consider a file named PROPERTY.DBF which is located in a sub-directory named Housing. This sub-directory is a sub-directory of Test, which in turn is a sub-directory of the main directory (that is, 'root' directory). The full name of the file would be C:\TEST\HOUSING\PROPERTY.DBF. The sub-directory in which PROPERTY.DBF is located would be called C:\TEST\HOUSING. The C: in this example is the identifying letter of the disk drive.

11

dBASE would make a sub-directory called \TEST\HOUSING. All the tables in the database would be stored in this sub-directory, along with a number of **catalogue tables**. These are special tables which dBASE uses to keep track of the data in the database.

In order to keep track of all the databases in the system, dBASE IV maintains one further database, called SQLHOME.

3.5 Entering SQL commands

In dBASE IV/SQL, there are two methods of entering commands. The simplest it to type the command at the SQL prompt. You type the command on a single line, with each part of the command following the preceding one, for example:

```
SELECT * FROM Sales WHERE Price > 4500;
```

The line will automatically scroll horizontally if the command is wider than the screen, up to a maximum of 254 characters. To execute the command, press the Enter key.

The other method is to press Ctrl-Home to open a text-editing window. You can type a command into this window, and you can space it out in any way you wish, including spreading it over several lines, for example:

```
SELECT *
FROM Sales
WHERE Price > 4500;
```

When using the text-editing window, the command may be up to 1024 characters long. When you have finished entering the command, press Ctrl-End. dBASE IV then executes the command. Using the text-editing window in this way makes it much easier to read commands, especially long ones.

Throughout this book, SQL commands are printed on several lines. This is done purely to make the commands easier to read.

If dBASE IV/SQL finds a mistake in a command, it displays a menu. This menu offers the following choices:

(a)   Cancel: ignore the command;
(b)   Edit: allow the command to be corrected;
(c)   Help: display a help screen which explains the syntax of the command.

Figure 3.3 shows an example of a user error: the omission of the

12

semicolon at the end of the command. In this case, the easiest way of dealing with the error would be to choose Edit and then correct the command.

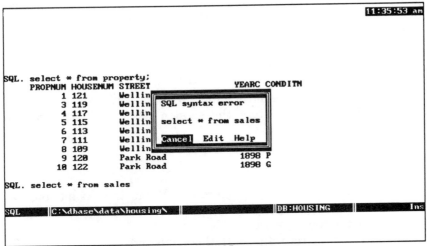

Fig. 3.3 dBASE IV/SQL error message.

Using the cursor-control keys, you can position the cursor at the point in the command line where the correction is to be made. You can then over-type the erroneous characters with new ones. It is also possible to type new characters into the middle of the line. To do this, go into **insert mode** by pressing the Ins key. The message 'ins' will appear on the screen. Press Ins a second time to come out of insert mode.

You can also call up the text-editing window to correct a command (by pressing Ctrl-Home).

3.5.1 The command history

It is also possible to recall the SQL commands which you typed earlier in the session. Pressing the up-arrow key brings the previous command to the screen; pressing the key again recalls the command before the previous one; and so on.

You can edit these commands in the usual way, including pressing the Ins key to switch between over-typing and inserting. Press the Enter key to execute the command.

By using both the down-arrow and up-arrow keys in this way, you can browse through all the commands which you have previously entered.

13

3.6 Saving your work

It is often useful to keep a record of a dBASE IV/SQL session, that is, of all the commands which you type and the results which they produce. To do this, first issue a command like the following (be sure to do this **before** you issue any of the commands which you want to save):

```
SET ALTERNATE TO Mywork.Txt
```

This establishes the name of a file – Mywork.Txt in this example – which will be used to store the session details. Next, type the following command:

```
SET ALTERNATE ON
```

This actually starts the recording. From this point on, all commands which you type, and all the results from the commands, will be saved in the Mywork.Txt file.

You can stop the recording with this command:

```
SET ALTERNATE OFF
```

You can continue to turn the recording on and off in the same way for as long as the file is open. However, you cannot do anything further with the file until it is closed. This is accomplished with the command:

```
CLOSE ALTERNATE
```

You can now examine the file, for example by using dBASE IV's built-in text editor as follows:

```
MODIFY FILE Mywork.Txt
```

When you have finished looking at the file, you can leave the text editor by press the Esc key (use Esc to close the editor only if nothing has been altered; Appendix A gives more information about using the editor).

The file can also be printed (after it has been closed), for example with a command such as:

```
TYPE Mywork.Txt TO PRINT
```

14

One important point about the SET ALTERNATE TO command: if a file with the specified name already exists, it will be overwritten by the new file. If this is not what you want, be sure to choose a different file name. If you want to append the new information to the end of an existing file, issue the following command:

```
SET ALTERNATE TO Myfile.Txt ADDITIVE
```

3.7 Closing down

The quickest way of leaving dBASE IV/SQL is with the command:

```
QUIT
```

This terminates the program and returns control to the operating system. You do not have to worry about closing individual files. dBASE IV/SQL does this for you.

If you only want to close a database – for example, in order to open another database – issue the following command:

```
STOP DATABASE;
```

3.8 The dBASE and SQL languages

At this point, we have to deal with a slight complication.

The capabilities of SQL are, to a large extent, limited to data manipulation (searching, adding and altering data) and data definition (creating databases and tables, and performing certain high-level operations on them). However, a sophisticated DBMS like dBASE IV can do a great deal more. We have already seen one small example: its ability to save a record of the session in a file. SQL has no command for achieving this. Because of SQL's limited functionality, designers of database management systems are forced to provide additional commands to make up for those which SQL lacks.

In the case of dBASE IV/SQL, it is the dBASE language which fills this gap. This is more or less the same language which is used with older versions of dBASE which do not support SQL.

The commands SET ALTERNATE TO and SET ALTERNATE ON are not part of SQL. Rather, they form part of the dBASE language. The same applies to the QUIT command which is used to end the dBASE IV session.

It is very easy to distinguish between SQL and dBASE commands:

15

SQL commands always end with a semi-colon; dBASE commands never do. dBASE IV/SQL will not execute an SQL command if you forget the semi-colon.

You might find it annoying, when learning SQL, to have to face the complexities of yet another language. But, in order to experiment with SQL (in the dBASE environment), you do need to know at least a few dBASE commands.

3.9 The structure of SQL commands

SQL commands are made up of the following elements: keywords; names defined by the user, such as the names of tables, columns and files; values; and operators.

In the following command:

```
SELECT *
FROM Sales
WHERE Price > 45000;
```

the keywords are SELECT, FROM and WHERE. Sales and Price are user-defined names. The figure 45000 is a constant and the '>' symbol is an operator. Keywords may not themselves be used as user-defined names.

Throughout this book, we follow the convention of printing keywords in capitals and user-defined names in mixed capitals and lower case. This is done purely to make it easier to understand the commands. dBASE IV/SQL does not itself care what combination of capitals or lower case is used.

In SQL, every command explicitly states what data it is working with. In the above example, the command specifies: the Sales table; every column; and those rows where the price exceeds £45,000.

CHAPTER FOUR

Setting up a database

4.1 Introduction

In the previous chapter, we saw how to set up a new, empty database by means of a command such as:

```
CREATE DATABASE Name;
```

However, before you can put any data into a new database, you must first set up some tables.

The first step is to decide the names which you are going to give to the tables and their columns. It is a good idea to choose names which help make the meanings of the tables and columns obvious (e.g. Property, Street). Table names are subject to a maximum of eight characters; column names may contain up to ten characters.

Each column must have a specific **data type**. dBASE IV/SQL has to know in advance whether a column is to be used for text, numbers, dates or whatever.

The chapter starts with a summary of the data types which dBASE IV/SQL recognises. After that, we will look at the method of defining tables and of entering data into them.

4.2 Data types

dBASE IV/SQL recognises the following data types:

(a) CHAR(n). Any kind of text. The number between the brackets indicates the maximum length of the data item; this may not exceed 254 characters. The data may contain any type of characters, including letters, digits, spaces and special symbols. An example: IBM-PC: 640K.

(b) SMALLINT. Whole numbers between -99 999 and 999 999.

(c) INTEGER. Positive whole numbers with up to 11 digits, or negative whole numbers with up to 10 digits.

17

(d) NUMERIC(x,y). Numbers which include a decimal point. y represents the number of digits after the decimal point; x is the total number of digits, including the sign and decimal point. The maximum value of x is 20; y can be between 0 and 18.

(e) DECIMAL(x,y). The same as NUMERIC except that x does not include the decimal point.

(f) FLOAT(x,y). Floating-point numbers in the range 0.1 E -307 to 0.9 E +308, expressed in exponential format. x represents the total number of digits, including the sign and decimal point, and must be between 1 to 20; y is the number of digits after the decimal point, in the range 0 to 18. An example of a floating-point number: 0.8 E +199.

(g) LOGICAL. Holds one of two values: true or false.

(h) DATE. Ordinary calendar dates.

4.3 Defining tables

The command for defining a new table consists of the keywords CREATE TABLE, followed by the name of the table, followed (in brackets) by a list of the column names and their respective data types.

The following command creates the Property table in our example database:

```
CREATE TABLE Property
(PropNum INTEGER, HouseNum CHAR(6), Street CHAR(20),
YearC SMALLINT, Conditn CHAR(1));
```

Although house numbers are generally numeric, we specify a CHAR type for the HouseNum column so as to cater for numbers such as 170A.

Similarly, the Sales table can be created like this:

```
CREATE TABLE Sales
(PropNum INTEGER, SaleDate DATE, Price INTEGER,
Buyer CHAR(20), Seller CHAR(20));
```

4.4 Adding rows

There are several ways of adding data to a table. One method is to add data row by row. This is achieved with the INSERT command.

The following command adds a single row to the property table:

18

```
INSERT INTO Property
VALUES (1,'Wellington St.','121',1899,'A');
```

The order in which the values appear in the command must correspond to the order of the columns within the table.

The way in which the values are expressed depends on the data type, as follows:

(a)   CHAR. PropNum, HouseNum, Street and Conditn are examples of CHARs. Values for this data type must always be entered between single quote marks.

(b)   SMALLINT, INTEGER, NUMERIC, DECIMAL and FLOAT. YearC is an example of a SMALLINT. When entering any of these values, **do not** use quote marks.

(c)   LOGICAL. Here, only two possible values are allowed: true and false. True values are represented as .T. or .Y., false values as .F. or .N. The full stops are obligatory; do not use quote marks.

(d)   DATE. Dates are entered as characters between braces, for example: {2/11/88}. SQL follows the same date settings as dBASE. In this book, we will assume that the date is set to British format and that centuries appear as two digits. The above date therefore represents 2nd November 1988.[1]

The INSERT command, when used as in the above example, can only add one row at a time to the table. If you want to add further rows, you may re-issue the command, using different values each time. A convenient way of doing this is to type the first INSERT command in full, then use the up-arrow key to bring it back to the screen. You can then edit the command, inserting the new values in place of the previous ones. Press Enter to execute the command. Each time that you do this, a new row will be added to the table.

---

[1]You can alter the way that dBASE displays dates by means of two commands in the Config.Db file. DATE = DMY stipulates that the day is to appear before the month and that the month is to appear before the year. The other possibilities are MDY and YMD. CENTURY = OFF says that the year should be shown as two digits. CENTURY = ON would display the year as four digits. The settings only affect the appearance of dates, not the way they are stored internally.

CHAPTER FIVE

Single-table searches

SQL offers many different options for retrieving information from a table. Data can be selected and sorted in various ways. It can also be summarised and grouped, and calculations can be carried out on it. In this chapter, we will take a closer look at these facilities as far as working with a single table is concerned.

5.1 The SELECT command

The result of every search or query is itself a table. This table is called a **result table**. A basic query specifies two characteristics of the result table: the criterion on which records will be selected for inclusion; and the columns which will appear.

You can think of a query as a sort of cut-and-paste operation, taking a portion of the original table and making it into a new result table. SQL does this by means of a single command: the SELECT command.

Throughout this chapter, we will use our Sales table as an example. Here is the complete table, showing the names of the columns:

PROP-NUM	SALE-DATE	PRICE	BUYER	SELLER
1	25/02/80	25000	FX Properties Ltd	P Johnson
6	01/12/81	22500	Vista Estates Ltd	T Taylor
1	26/02/80	40000	Vista Estates Ltd	FX Properties Ltd
1	27/02/80	50000	Ballerton D.C.	Vista Estates Ltd
3	11/11/81	17500	Ballerton D.C.	T Zander
8	01/01/82	20000	Vista Estates Ltd	L Lauder
9	30/01/82	30000	Vista Estates Ltd	W Bendix
10	05/05/83	35000	FX Properties Ltd	I Stevenson
10	22/05/83	37500	Vista Estates Ltd	FX Properties Ltd

20

In this table, the columns headed PropNum and Price are NUMERIC data types; the SaleDate column is a DATE type; and the Buyer and Seller columns are both of type CHAR.

In order to view the entire table, we use the command:

```
SELECT *
FROM Sales;
```

The asterisk in this command means 'all columns'. The following command would produce an identical result:

```
SELECT PropNum, SaleDate, Price, Buyer, Seller
FROM Sales;
```

The names which follow the keyword SELECT are the columns which are to be displayed. By specifying column names in this way, you make a sort of 'vertical selection'. Any columns which you do not specify are ignored. The column names must be separated by commas.

The following command displays the buyers and sellers for each sale:

```
SELECT Buyer, Seller
FROM Sales;
```

The result of this query would be:

BUYER	SELLER
FX Properties Ltd	P Johnson
Vista Estates Ltd	T Taylor
Vista Estates Ltd	FX Properties Ltd
Ballerton D.C.	Vista Estates Ltd
Ballerton D.C.	T Zander
Vista Estates Ltd	L Lauder
Vista Estates Ltd	W Bendix
FX Properties Ltd	I Stevenson
Vista Estates Ltd	FX Properties Ltd

In order to do anything useful with the SELECT command, you need to know which tables are present in the database, and which columns make up each of the tables. This information is itself stored in special tables called **catalogue tables**. Section 6.13 describes how to view the information in catalogue tables.

21

5.2 Eliminating duplicates

By adding the keyword DISTINCT to a query, we can eliminate duplicate records from the result.

Query: Who are the buyers of the properties in the table?

```
SELECT DISTINCT Buyer
FROM Sales;
```

Result:

```
BUYER
FX Properties Ltd
Vista Estates Ltd
Ballerton D.C.
```

5.3 Sorting

If you want to show the results of a query in a particular order, add an ORDER BY clause to the SELECT command. This consists of the keywords ORDER BY, followed by the name of the field on which you want the results to be sorted. To specify the direction of the sort, add either ASC or DESC, for ascending and descending order respectively. If you do not specify the direction, the results will be in ascending order.

Query: Show all the sellers in alphabetical order.

```
SELECT DISTINCT Seller
FROM Sales
ORDER BY Seller ASC;
```

Result:

```
SELLER
Bendix, W
FX Properties Ltd
Johnson, P
Lauder, L
Stevenson, I
Taylor, T
Vista Estates Ltd
Zander, T
```

22

Or the other way round:

```
SELECT DISTINCT Seller
FROM Sales
ORDER BY Seller DESC;
```

Resulting in:

```
SELLER
Zander, T
Vista Estates Ltd
Taylor, T
Stevenson, I
Lauder, L
Johnson, P
FX Properties Ltd
Bendix, W
```

It is also possible to have one sort 'inside' another.

Query: For each transaction, list the buyer and the price, in buyer order; within each buyer, show the transactions in descending order of price.

```
SELECT Buyer, Price
FROM Sales
ORDER BY Buyer ASC, Price DESC;
```

Result:

```
BUYER                PRICE
Ballerton D.C.       50000
Ballerton D.C.       17500
FX Properties Ltd    35000
FX Properties Ltd    25000
Vista Estates Ltd    40000
Vista Estates Ltd    37500
Vista Estates Ltd    30000
Vista Estates Ltd    22500
Vista Estates Ltd    20000
```

The various components (or **clauses**) of the SELECT command must appear in a definite order. First comes the keyword SELECT, followed by the list of columns which are to appear in the result. This is followed by the FROM clause, which specifies the name of the table being used. Next comes the WHERE clause, if any (this is described in the next section). After that comes any ORDER BY clause for specifying the sorting order.

Query: Give the buyers and prices for all transactions where more than £30,000 was spent. Show the result in buyer sequence.

```
SELECT Buyer, Price
FROM Sales
WHERE Price > 30000
ORDER BY Buyer;
```

Result:

BUYER	PRICE
Ballerton D.C.	50000
FX Properties Ltd	35000
Vista Estates Ltd	40000
Vista Estates Ltd	37500

5.4 Selecting rows

To select rows from a table, you have to specify a **condition**. The result table will consist of data from each row that meets the condition. You specify the condition by adding a WHERE clause to the SELECT command.

Query: Give the property number and price of all properties which have been sold for more than £25,000.

```
SELECT PropNum, Price
FROM Sales
WHERE Price > 25000;
```

Result:

PROPNUM	PRICE
1	40000
1	50000
9	30000
10	35000
10	37500

You can think of this SELECT command as a combination of

horizontal and vertical selections. The horizontal selection stipulates the rows to be selected: in this case, those where the price exceeds £25,000. Here is the original table:

PROP-NUM	SALE-DATE	PRICE	BUYER	SELLER
1	25/02/80	25000	FX Properties Ltd	P Johnson
6	01/12/81	22500	Vista Estates Ltd	T Taylor
*1	26/02/80	40000	Vista Estates Ltd	FX Properties Ltd
*1	27/02/80	50000	Ballerton D.C.	Vista Estates Ltd
3	11/11/81	17500	Ballerton D.C.	T Zander
8	01/01/82	20000	Vista Estates Ltd	L Lauder
*9	30/01/82	30000	Vista Estates Ltd	W Bendix
*10	05/05/83	35000	FX Properties Ltd	I Stevenson
*10	22/05/83	37500	Vista Estates Ltd	FX Properties Ltd

The asterisks in the above table indicate the rows which meet the condition. After the query has been performed, the following result table will appear:

PROP-NUM	SALE-DATE	PRICE	BUYER	SELLER
1	26/02/80	40000	Vista Estates Ltd	FX Properties Ltd
1	27/02/80	50000	Ballerton D.C.	Vista Estates Ltd
9	30/01/82	30000	Vista Estates Ltd	W Bendix
10	05/05/83	35000	FX Properties Ltd	I Stevenson
10	22/05/83	37500	Vista Estates Ltd	FX Properties Ltd

The vertical selection is the choice of columns which are to be displayed: property number and price in this example:

PROPNUM	PRICE
1	40000
1	50000
9	30000
10	35000
10	37500

The condition which appears in a WHERE clause generally involves some form of comparison or relationship. In the above example, the comparison is between the figure in the Price column and the value 25,000. The '>' (greater than) symbol used in the comparison is a **relational operator**.

25

The relational operators which SQL recognises are shown in Table 5.1. The way in which values are specified in these comparisons depends on the data. The same rules apply here as for the INSERT command (for example, using quotes for character data).

Table 5.1. Relational operators in SQL

Operator	Meaning
<	less than
>	greater than
!<	not less than
=	equal to
<=	less than or equal to
>=	greater than or equal to
!>	not greater than
<>	not equal to
!=	not equal to

5.4.1. CHAR-type data

Values of data type CHAR must be written between quotation marks. You may use either single or double quotation marks, provided that you do so consistently; that is, 'Vista Estates Ltd' and "Vista Estates Ltd" are both valid, but "Vista Estates Ltd' is not.

Query: Which properties were bought by purchasers other than by Vista Estates?

```
SELECT PropNum
FROM Sales
WHERE Buyer <> 'Vista Estates Ltd';
```

When comparing items of type CHAR, dBASE IV works on a strictly literal basis. For example, the Sales table contains data for a seller called Vista Estates Ltd. If you tried to locate this company using either of the following two commands, the search would fail:

```
SELECT *
FROM Sales
WHERE Seller = 'VISTA ESTATES LTD';

SELECT *
FROM Sales
WHERE Seller = ' Vista Estates Ltd ';
```

26

In the first case, SQL would look for records in which the seller's name was stored in capitals. In the second case, it would search for a name beginning and ending with a space. Since neither of these conditions apply to the actual data in the table, no records would be retrieved.

The following is the correct way to carry out this search:

```
SELECT *
FROM Sales
WHERE Seller = 'Vista Estates Ltd';
```

5.4.2 Numeric data

Numeric values – that is, data items of types SMALLINT, INTEGER, DECIMAL, NUMERIC and FLOAT – are entered **without** quotation marks.

Query: Which properties were sold for £25,000 or less?

```
SELECT PropNum, Price
FROM Sales
WHERE Price <= 25000;
```

Do not type commas or a currency symbol with the number. Decimal points and leading signs may be entered where permitted by the data type.

5.4.3 DATE-type data

Values of type DATE must be written between braces. The format of the date depends on how dBASE IV was installed. In this book, the DD/MM/YY format is used (e.g. 21st November 1992 would be entered as 21/11/92).[1]

Query: Which properties were sold in 1982 or later?

```
SELECT PropNum, SaleDate
FROM Sales
WHERE SaledDate >= {01/01/82};
```

Result:

PROPNUM	SALEDATE
8	01/01/82
9	30/01/82

---

[1]See note on page 19.

```
10        05/05/83
10        22/05/83
```

5.4.4 LOGICAL-type data

The two possible logical values are written as `.T.` and `.F.` (for True and False). If the Property table had a column called Renovated, we could find out which properties had been renovated by asking:

```
SELECT *
FROM Property
WHERE Renovated = .T.;
```

Furthermore, since Renovated is itself a logical **expression**, we could ask the same question like this:

```
SELECT *
FROM Property
WHERE Renovated;
```

dBASE has some flexibility in comparing data items of different types. In particular, the various numeric types (SMALLINT, INTEGER, DECIMAL, NUMERIC and FLOAT) may be compared with each other. However, CHAR values may only be compared with other CHAR values. Similarly, DATE and LOGICAL data may only be compared with data of their own type.

5.5 Combinations using AND, OR and NOT

By using the keywords AND, OR and NOT, it is possible to combine simple conditions to produce more complex ones. AND, OR and NOT are called **logical operators**.

Query: List the property numbers and buyers of those properties which were bought by either FX Properties or Vista Estates.

```
SELECT PropNum, Buyer
FROM Sales
WHERE Buyer = 'FX Properties Ltd'
OR Buyer = 'Vista Estates Ltd';
```

Result:

```
PROPNUM      BUYER
1            FX Properties Ltd
```

28

```
6          Vista Estates Ltd
1          Vista Estates Ltd
8          Vista Estates Ltd
9          Vista Estates Ltd
10         FX Properties Ltd
10         Vista Estates Ltd
```

When two conditions are combined with OR, the entire condition is considered true if either (or both) of the component conditions is true. This is shown in the **truth table** in Table 5.2.

Table 5.2. Truth table for OR

A	B	A OR B
true	true	true
true	false	true
false	true	true
false	false	false

When the conditions are combined with AND, both the component conditions must be true in order for the combined condition to be true. The truth table for AND is shown in Table 5.3.

Table 5.3. Truth table for AND

A	B	A AND B
true	true	true
true	false	false
false	true	false
false	false	false

Query: Give details of the properties which were sold by Vista Estates to Ballerton District Council.

```
SELECT PropNum, Price, Buyer, Seller
FROM Sales
WHERE Buyer = 'Ballerton D.C.'
AND Seller = 'Vista Estates Ltd';
```

Result:

PROPNUM	PRICE	BUYER	SELLER
1	50000	Ballerton D.C.	Vista Estates Ltd

Single-table searches

NOT reverses the result of a condition, as shown in Table 5.4.

Table 5.4 Truth table for NOT

A	NOT A
true	false
false	true

Query: List the property numbers and buyers of all sales where the buyer was not Ballerton District Council.

```
SELECT PropNum, Buyer
FROM Sales
WHERE NOT Buyer = 'Ballerton D.C.';
```

Result:

PROPNUM	BUYER
1	FX Properties Ltd
6	Vista Estates Ltd
1	Vista Estates Ltd
8	Vista Estates Ltd
9	Vista Estates Ltd
10	FX Properties Ltd
10	Vista Estates Ltd

It is possible to combine more than two conditions in this way.

Query: Which properties did Ballerton Council buy from Vista Estates before 1982?

```
SELECT *
FROM Sales
WHERE SaleDate < {01/01/82}
AND Buyer = 'Ballerton D.C.'
AND Seller = 'Vista Estates Ltd';
```

Result:

PROP-NUM	SALE-DATE	PRICE	BUYER	SELLER
1	27/02/80	50000	Ballerton D.C.	Vista Estates Ltd

When you combine conditions using different logical operators, a rule of precedence applies: NOT takes priority over AND which in turn takes priority over OR. But even if you know this rule, it is easy to create a complex expression which means something other than what you intended. The solution is to use parentheses to establish the order of evaluation.

Query: Which sales did not involve either FX Properties or Vista Estates, either as buyer or seller?

```
SELECT *
FROM Sales
WHERE NOT (Buyer = 'Vista Estates Ltd'
OR Seller = 'Vista Estates Ltd'
OR Buyer = 'FX Properties Ltd'
OR Seller = 'FX Properties Ltd');
```

Result:

PROP-NUM	SALE-DATE	PRICE	BUYER	SELLER
3	11/11/81	17500	Ballerton D.C.	T Zander

Query: Which properties did either Vista Estates or FX Properties buy for more than £25,000?

```
SELECT *
FROM Sales
WHERE Price > 25000
AND (Buyer = 'Vista Estates Ltd'
OR Buyer = 'FX Properties Ltd');
```

Result:

PROP-NUM	SALE-DATE	PRICE	BUYER	SELLER
1	26/02/80	40000	Vista Estates Ltd	FX Properties Ltd
9	30/01/82	30000	Vista Estates Ltd	W Bendix
10	05/05/83	35000	FX Properties Ltd	I Stevenson
10	22/05/83	37500	Vista Estates Ltd	FX Properties Ltd

5.6 Searching with patterns

It is often useful to be able to search for just part of a value, that is, for a string of characters that occurs anywhere within a target field.

You might do this, for example, if you did not know the exact name of the property company you were looking for, but you did know that the word Estates appeared somewhere in the name.

In SQL, it is possible to search for a **pattern**. You do this by means of the keyword LIKE. This keyword (or **predicate**) is used in conjunction with a character string which contains **wildcard** characters. An example of a wildcard character is the percentage sign; it is a single character which represents any other character. (You can use an asterisk as an alternative to the percentage sign.)

Query: Is there a buyer that has the word Estates somewhere in its name?

```
SELECT SaleDate, Price, Buyer, Seller
FROM Sales
WHERE Buyer LIKE '%Estates%';
```

Result:

SALEDATE	PRICE	BUYER	SELLER
01/12/81	22500	Vista Estates Ltd	T Taylor
26/02/80	40000	Vista Estates Ltd	FX Properties Ltd
01/01/82	20000	Vista Estates Ltd	L Lauder
30/01/82	30000	Vista Estates Ltd	W Bendix
22/05/83	37500	Vista Estates Ltd	FX Properties Ltd

The percentage sign can be used as a wildcard for an entire string of characters. Another wildcard character, the underscore character, represents exactly one other character. (The question mark is an alternative to the underscore.)

Query: Which sellers have 'a' as the fourth character of their names?

```
SELECT Seller
FROM Sales
WHERE Seller LIKE '___a%';
```

Result:

```
SELLER
T Taylor
T Zander
L Lauder
```

The following query is exactly the same:

32

```
SELECT Seller
FROM Sales
WHERE Seller LIKE '????a%*;
```

5.7 Calculated columns

The SELECT command can include calculations, based on the contents of columns. In the following example, dBASE IV/SQL displays each Price field increased by a factor of 1.2.

```
SELECT Price, Price * 1.2
FROM Sales;
```

Result:

```
PRICE        EXP1
25000        30000.00
22500        27000.00
40000        48000.00
50000        60000.00
17500        21000.00
20000        24000.00
30000        36000.00
35000        42000.00
37500        45000.00
```

dBASE IV/SQL itself generates the heading EXP1 to represent the first calculated column (or **expression**) in the result table.

The asterisk in the above command is used here as an **arithmetic operator**. There are five arithmetic operators in all. They are shown in Table 5.5.

In complex expressions, parentheses may be used to change the precedence of the operations.

Table 5.5. Arithmetic operators in SQL

Operator	Meaning
+	addition
–	subtraction
*	multiplication
/	division
** or ^	exponentiation

33

You may also use calculated columns to display fixed text in a result table. In the next example, one of the expressions consists simply of the word 'Increased'. The effect is to generate a column which contains the specified word in every row.

```
SELECT 'Increased', Price * 1.2
FROM Sales;
```

This produces:

EXP1	EXP2
Increased	30000.00
Increased	27000.00
Increased	48000.00
Increased	60000.00
Increased	21000.00
Increased	24000.00
Increased	36000.00
Increased	42000.00
Increased	45000.00

5.8 Selections based on ranges

The BETWEEN predicate can be used to simplify the selection of values that lie within a specified range.

Query: Which sales involved prices between £25,000 and £50,000?

```
SELECT SaleDate, Price, Buyer, Seller
FROM Sales
WHERE Price BETWEEN 25000 AND 50000;
```

The results are:

SALEDATE	PRICE	BUYER	SELLER
25/02/80	25000	FX Properties Ltd	P Johnson
26/02/80	40000	Vista Estates Ltd	FX Properties Ltd
27/02/80	50000	Ballerton D.C.	Vista Estates Ltd
30/01/82	30000	Vista Estates Ltd	W Bendix
05/05/83	35000	FX Properties Ltd	I Stevenson
22/05/83	37500	Vista Estates Ltd	FX Properties Ltd

Exactly the same results could be obtained by combining two separate conditions with the AND operator, as follows:

34

```
SELECT Price, SaleDate, Buyer, Seller
FROM Sales
WHERE Price >= 25000 AND Price <=50000;
```

5.9 Aggregate functions

SQL makes it easy to obtain **aggregate** information from tables. Special functions are used to calculate totals and averages, to count rows, and to find minimum and maximum values.

The SUM function is used to find totals.

Query: What is the total prices in all Sales transactions?

```
SELECT SUM (Price)
FROM Sales;
```

Result:

```
        SUM1
277500.00
```

You can also limit the totalling to those rows which meet some specific condition. This is done by adding a WHERE clause.

Query: What is the total amount which FX Properties has received for the properties which it has sold?

```
SELECT SUM (Price)
FROM Sales
WHERE Seller LIKE 'FX%';
```

The answer is:

```
       SUM1
77500.00
```

In order to produce a count of rows, we use the COUNT(*) function (note the asterisk between the parentheses). The function counts the number of rows in the result table.

Query: How many properties were sold for more than £25,000?

```
SELECT COUNT(*)
FROM Sales
WHERE Price > 25000;
```

35

Result:

```
COUNT1
 5.00
```

A variation of this function is to add the keyword DISTINCT followed by a column name. This yields the number of distinct values in the specified column.

Query: How many different buyers are there?

```
SELECT COUNT (DISTINCT Buyers)
FROM Sales;
```

The answer is:

```
COUNT1
 3.00
```

The MAX function enables us to find the highest value in a column.

Query: What is the highest price in the Sales table?

```
SELECT MAX(Price)
FROM Sales;
```

Result:

```
   MAX1
50000.00
```

And, as you would expect, MIN finds the lowest value present.

Query: What is the lowest price in the Sales table?

```
SELECT MIN(Price)
FROM Sales;
```

Result:

```
   MIN1
17500.00
```

The AVG function is used to find the mean average of the values in a specified column.

Aggregates with grouping

Query: What is the average selling price?

```
SELECT AVG(Price)
FROM Sales;
```

Result:

```
      AVG1
  30833.33
```

Any or all of the aggregate functions can be combined in a single command, as in the next example:

```
SELECT COUNT(*),
MAX(Price), MIN(Price), AVG(Price), SUM(Price),
FROM Sales
WHERE Buyer = 'Vista Estates Ltd';
```

This produces:

COUNT1	MAX2	MIN3	AVG4	SUM5
5	40000.00	20000.00	30000.00	150000.00

5.10 Aggregates with grouping

It is possible to apply the aggregate functions to **groups** of rows. For example, suppose that we wanted to know the average price paid by each buyer. We can achieve this by adding a GROUP BY clause to the SELECT command.

Query: What is the average price per buyer?

```
SELECT Buyer, AVG(Price)
FROM Sales
GROUP BY Buyer;
```

The reply table shows as at a glance that the district council has paid the most money per property:

G_BUYER	AVG1
FX Properties Ltd	30000.00
Ballerton D.C.	33750.00
Vista Estates Ltd	30000.00

Whatever column names are included in the GROUP BY clause must also appear in the list of columns immediately after the word SELECT.

Going further, we can restrict the output from this kind of command to certain groups. By adding a HAVING clause, we can specify a condition which each group must meet in order to appear in the result table. This is shown in the next example.

Query: Give the average price per buyer for all buyers who have spent more than £40,000 on a single property.

```
SELECT Buyer, AVG(Price)
FROM Sales
GROUP BY Buyer
HAVING MAX(Price) > 40000;
```

Result:

```
G_BUYER                    AVG1
Ballerton D.C.        33750.00
```

Two rules to note: you **must** include at least one of the aggregate functions (SUM, COUNT(*), AVG, MIN or MAX) in the HAVING clause; and you cannot include a HAVING clause unless there is also a GROUP BY clause.

The difference between HAVING and WHERE is that HAVING imposes a condition on a **group**. The WHERE clause applies the condition to individual rows.

In the final example, HAVING and WHERE are combined.

Query: Give the average price per buyer, for all buyers whose average price exceeds £25,000. Limit the selection to buyers who are companies ('Ltd' appears in the name).

```
SELECT Buyer, AVG(Price)
FROM Sales
WHERE Buyer LIKE '*Ltd*'
HAVING AVG(Price) > 25000;
```

Result:

```
G_BUYER                    AVG1
FX Properties Ltd     30000.00
Vista Estates Ltd     30000.00
```

CHAPTER SIX

Multiple-table searches

6.1 Introduction

In the previous chapter, we saw how to obtain information from a database by searching one table at a time. However, SQL does not really come into its own until you perform queries involving two or more tables.

Our example Housing database contains two tables:

```
Property table:
```

PROPNUM	HOUSENUM	STREET	YEARC	CONDITN
1	121	Wellington St.	1899	A
2	123	Wellington St.	1899	A
3	119	Wellington St.	1899	A
4	117	Wellington St.	1899	A
5	115	Wellington St.	1899	P
6	113	Wellington St.	1898	P
7	111	Wellington St.	1898	P
8	109	Wellington St.	1898	P
9	120	Park Road	1898	P
10	122	Park Road	1898	G

```
Sales table:
```

PROP-NUM	SALE-DATE	PRICE	BUYER	SELLER
1	25/02/80	25000	FX Properties Ltd	P Johnson
6	01/12/81	22500	Vista Estates Ltd	T Taylor
1	26/02/80	40000	Vista Estates Ltd	FX Properties Ltd
1	27/02/80	50000	Ballerton D.C.	Vista Estates Ltd
3	11/11/81	17500	Ballerton D.C.	T Zander
8	01/01/82	20000	Vista Estates Ltd	L Lauder
9	30/01/82	30000	Vista Estates Ltd	W Bendix

```
10   05/05/83 35000 FX Properties Ltd  I Stevenson
10   22/05/83 37500 Vista Estates Ltd  FX Properties Ltd
```

You can only query two tables at the same time if the tables are linked by means of a common value. In this example, the link is effected by the value of the property number. If a row in the Property table represents property number x, the corresponding rows in the Sales table also have a property number x. (In this case, the two tables have the same column names, PropNum, but this is not essential. It is the **value** which must be common to the tables, not the name.)

The link between the Property and Sales table is shown diagrammatically in Fig. 6.1. The line between the PropNum columns in the two tables represents the linking value.

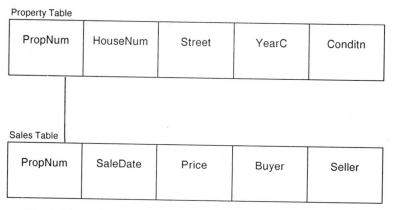

Fig. 6.1 How the two tables in the Housing database are linked.

In this chapter, we will use the same linked tables to examine ways of performing multiple-table queries.

6.2 Joins

We have seen that the Property table and the Sales table can be linked by means of the contents of the two PropNum fields. In database terminology, this kind of linkage is called a **join**.

A join between two tables can be thought of as a new, wider table. This new table contains all the columns from both of the original tables.

The join table contains a row for each of the rows in one of the original tables combined with each of the rows in the other original table — but only in as far as that represents a sensible relationship.

What constitutes a sensible relationship? The answer depends on the nature of the data in the linking columns.

In our example database, a 'sensible relationship' exists when the two sets of data relate to the same property, that is, when the linking columns (PropNum) contain the same property number. So the join table will contain a row for each row in the Property table combined with each row in the Sales table that has the same PropNum.

Let's look at the join table row by row. The first row is formed from the first row of the Property table and the first row of the Sales table, since these both have a property number of 1. This row has the following data (the values have been abbreviated here in order to fit on the page):

Prop	No Str	Year	Cond	Prop	SaleDate	Price	Buyer	Seller
1	121 W.S.	1899	A	1	25/2/80	25000	FX	Johnsn

The second row of the join table is formed from the first row of Property and the third row of Sales, as these too share a PropNum of 1. Similarly, the third row of the join is formed from the first row of Property and the fourth row of Sales. Here then are the first three rows of the join:

Prop	No Str	Year	Cond	Prop	SaleDate	Price	Buyer	Seller
1	121 W.S.	1899	A	1	25/2/80	25000	FX	Johnsn
1	121 W.S.	1899	A	1	26/2/80	40000	Vista	FX
1	121 W.S.	1899	A	1	27/2/80	50000	Baltn	Vista

There are no further rows in the Sales table for property number 1, so we can move on to the second row of the Property table. Here the PropNum is 2. But there are no sales for property number 2, so this row does not contribute anything to the join. The third row of the Property table (PropNum = 3), on the other hand, does have a sale: shown in the sixth row of the Sales table. So these two rows form the fourth row of the join. Further rows are added to the join in the same way. The complete join is as follows:

Prop	No Str	Year	Cond	Prop	SaleDate	Price	Buyer	Seller
1	121 W.S.	1899	A	1	25/02/80	25000	FX	Johnsn
1	121 W.S.	1899	A	1	26/02/80	40000	Vista	FX
1	121 W.S.	1899	A	1	27/02/80	50000	Baltn	Vista
3	119 W.S.	1899	A	3	11/11/81	17500	Baltn	Zander
6	113 W.S.	1898	P	6	01/12/81	22500	Vista	Taylor
8	109 W.S.	1898	P	8	01/01/82	20000	Vista	Lauder

```
 9    120 P.R. 1898  P   9    30/01/82 30000 Vista Bendix
10    122 P.R. 1898  G  10    05/05/83 35000 FX    Stvnsn
10    122 P.R. 1898  G  10    22/05/83 37500 Vista FX
```

In order to create this join in SQL, you could issue the following command:

```
SELECT *
FROM Property, Sales
WHERE Property.PropNum = Sales.PropNum;
```

The FROM clause specifies the names of the tables from which the join is formed. The WHERE clause defines the condition under which the rows from the two tables will be combined.

If the same column name appears in both tables (as is the case here with PropNum), the column name must be preceded by the table name and separated from it by a full stop. If this is not done, SQL will reject the command.

If no join condition is specified, as is the case in the following example:

```
SELECT *
FROM Property, Sales;
```

then every row from the first table would be combined with every row from the second table. Clearly, this would be meaningless.

Joins help us to obtain answers to many kinds of queries. Let's look at some examples.

Query: Which properties (property number, house number and street name) have been sold and for how much?

```
SELECT Property.PropNum, HouseNum, Street, Price
FROM Property, Sales
WHERE Property.PropNum = Sales.PropNum;
```

Result:

PropNum	HouseNum	Street	Price
1	121	Wellington St.	25000
1	121	Wellington St.	40000
1	121	Wellington St.	50000
3	119	Wellington St.	17500
6	113	Wellington St.	22500

8	109	Wellington St.	20000
9	120	Park Road	30000
10	122	Park Road	35000
10	122	Park Road	37500

In the above SQL command, the join table will contain four columns from the two component tables.

Since the PropNum column occurs in both of the original tables, we have to precede its name with the table name and a full stop. If this was not done, SQL would reject the command with the message 'Ambiguous column name'. SQL never accepts any sort of ambiguity in a command.

The fact that there is more than one table name listed in the FROM clause tells SQL that the result table is to be a join.

The WHERE clause specifies the criterion on which the rows in the two tables will be combined. In this case,

```
WHERE Property.PropNum = Sales.PropNum
```

stipulates that the records from the Property table will be combined with those from the Sales table where the two tables have the same values in the PropNum columns.

It is not necessary for the columns which appear in the linking condition to have the same names. The linking is established on the basis of the **contents** of the fields, not their names.

The results of a multi-table query can be sorted in exactly the same way as with a single table.

Query: Which properties (property number, house number and street name) have been sold and for how much? Show the results in price order.

```
SELECT Property.PropNum, HouseNum, Street, Price
FROM Property, Sales
WHERE Property.PropNum = Sales.PropNum
ORDER BY Price;
```

Result:

PropNum	HouseNum	Street	Price
3	119	Wellington St.	17500
8	109	Wellington St.	20000
6	113	Wellington St.	22500
1	121	Wellington St.	25000

9	120	Park Road	30000
10	122	Park Road	35000
10	122	Park Road	37500
1	121	Wellington St.	40000
1	121	Wellington St.	50000

In this example, no condition was specified for selecting rows, apart from the join condition. If you do want to specify one or more criteria for selecting rows, you can simply add them to the WHERE clause.

Query: When and for how much was 121 Wellington Street sold?

```
SELECT SaleDate, Price
FROM Property, Sales
WHERE Property.PropNum = Sales.PropNum
AND HouseNum = '121'
AND Street = 'Wellington St.';
```

Result:

SALES->SALEDATE	SALES->PRICE
25/02/80	25000
26/02/80	40000
27/02/80	50000

6.2.1 The outer join (This section can be skipped on a first reading.)

Suppose that we want to extract all the information in the database concerning Wellington Street. It would be nice to be able to create a query which gave rise to the following result table:

Prop	No	Str	Year	Cond	Prop	SaleDate	Price	Buyer	Seller
1	121	W.S.	1899	A	1	25/02/80	25000	FX	Johnsn
1	121	W.S.	1899	A	1	26/02/80	40000	Vista	FX
1	121	W.S.	1899	A	1	27/02/80	50000	Baltn	Vista
3	119	W.S.	1899	A	3	11/11/81	17500	Baltn	Zander
6	113	W.S.	1898	P	6	01/12/81	22500	Vista	Taylor
8	109	W.S.	1898	P	8	01/01/82	20000	Vista	Lauder
2	123	W.S.	1899	A					
4	117	W.S.	1899	A					
5	115	W.S.	1899	P					
7	111	W.S.	1898	P					

Unfortunately, it is not possible to obtain this result in SQL with a single command. The only way of doing it is to form two separate queries. First, you would ask for data concerning those properties which **have** been sold:

```
SELECT *
FROM Property, Sales
WHERE Property.PropNum = Sales.PropNum
AND Street = 'Wellington St.';
```

You would than ask for information about the properties which have **not** been sold:

```
SELECT *
FROM Property
WHERE Street = 'Wellington St.'
AND PropNum NOT IN
   (SELECT PropNum FROM Sales);
```

An ordinary join contains information from only those rows which meet the join condition. So by joining the Property table with the Sales table, we can only get information about properties which have been sold. An **outer join** would contain these same rows; but it would also contain data from rows in the Property table which do not have corresponding rows in the Sales table. The missing items would simply be left blank. However, neither standard SQL nor dBASE IV/SQL supports the outer join.

6.3 Alternative names

Entering complex SQL commands often involves considerable typing. You can reduce this typing somewhat by using alternative table names, or **aliases**. This is shown in the following example.

Query: Which properties (property number, house number and street name) have been sold and for how much?

```
SELECT P.PropNum, HouseNum, Street, Price
FROM Property P, Sales S
WHERE P.PropNum = S.PropNum;
```

Result:

P->PropNum	P->HouseNum	P->Street	S->Price
1	121	Wellington St.	25000

45

1	121	Wellington St.	40000
1	121	Wellington St.	50000
3	119	Wellington St.	17500
6	113	Wellington St.	22500
8	109	Wellington St.	20000
9	120	Park Road	30000
10	122	Park Road	35000
10	122	Park Road	37500

In the FROM clause, each table name is followed by a letter. These letters can be used elsewhere in the command in place of the column names. Thus P.PropNum is the same as Property.PropNum.

You may not use the letters A to J as aliases. dBASE IV reserves these letters for its own work area aliases.

6.3.1 Joining a table with itself

A good way of using aliases is to create a join between a table and itself. This might sound odd. However, in principle a join can be made between completely arbitrary tables, so there is no reason why we cannot join a table with a copy of the same table. This is called a **self-join**.

For certain kinds of queries, a self-join is often the most convenient method of obtaining an answer.

In the Sales table, there are a number of properties which were bought by a property company and which were re-sold some time later. Suppose that we wished to find out how much profit these sales generated. In dealing with such a query, it would be useful to have a table of those properties which were bought and re-sold, showing their buying and selling prices.

We can create this table by making a join between the Sales table and a copy of itself. We can do this in such a way that the seller in one table equates to the buyer in the other.

The following command creates the self-join:

```
SELECT X.Price, X.Buyer, Y.Price, Y.Seller
FROM Sales X, Sales Y
WHERE X.PropNum = Y.PropNum
AND X.Buyer = Y.Seller;
```

The result would be:

X->PRICE	X->BUYER	Y->PRICE	Y->SELLER
25000	FX Properties Ltd	40000	FX Properties Ltd

46

| 40000 | Vista Estates Ltd | 50000 | Vista Estates Ltd |
| 35000 | FX Properties Ltd | 37500 | FX Properties Ltd |

The trick is to use two different aliases (X and Y in this example) for the Sales table. We could then proceed with the query as if we had two separate but identical tables. Table X would be:

PROP-NUM	SALE-DATE	PRICE	BUYER	SELLER
1	25/02/80	25000	FX Properties Ltd	P Johnson
6	01/12/81	22500	Vista Estates Ltd	T Taylor
1	26/02/80	40000	Vista Estates Ltd	FX Properties Ltd
1	27/02/80	50000	Ballerton D.C.	Vista Estates Ltd
3	11/11/81	17500	Ballerton D.C.	T Zander
8	01/01/82	20000	Vista Estates Ltd	L Lauder
9	30/01/82	30000	Vista Estates Ltd	W Bendix
10	05/05/83	35000	FX Properties Ltd	I Stevenson
10	22/05/83	37500	Vista Estates Ltd	FX Properties Ltd

and Table Y would be:

PROP-NUM	SALE-DATE	PRICE	BUYER	SELLER
1	25/02/80	25000	FX Properties Ltd	P Johnson
6	01/12/81	22500	Vista Estates Ltd	T Taylor
1	26/02/80	40000	Vista Estates Ltd	FX Properties Ltd
1	27/02/80	50000	Ballerton D.C.	Vista Estates Ltd
3	11/11/81	17500	Ballerton D.C.	T Zander
8	01/01/82	20000	Vista Estates Ltd	L Lauder
9	30/01/82	30000	Vista Estates Ltd	W Bendix
10	05/05/83	35000	FX Properties Ltd	I Stevenson
10	22/05/83	37500	Vista Estates Ltd	FX Properties Ltd

It is perfectly possible to make a join between Table X and Table Y. A row in Table X is combined with a row in Table Y if the two rows have the same property number and if the buyer in Table X is the same as the seller in Table Y. The result table therefore has one row for each case in which a given entity has both bought and sold the same property.

The first row in Table X has FX Properties as its buyer. This row would be combined with the third row of Table Y. In order to obtain the information we want from the linkage, the result table would require the following columns: X.Price, X.Buyer, Y.Price and Y.Buyer. The first row in the results table would therefore be as follows:

```
X->PRICE   X->BUYER            Y->PRICE  Y->SELLER
25000      FX Properties Ltd   40000     FX Properties Ltd
```

dBASE IV/SQL would then look to see if it could combine the first row in Table X with another row in Table Y. This is not possible. So it proceeds to the second row of X, looking in turn at each row in Y to see if it is eligible for joining. It continues in the same way, creating a row in the results table for each combination of rows which meets the two conditions.

Since we want to see at a glance the total profit made by each company, we will issue the following command:

```
SELECT SUM(Y.Price - X.Price), X.Buyer
FROM Sales X, Sales Y
WHERE X.PropNum = Y.PropNum
AND X.Buyer = Y.Seller
GROUP BY X.Buyer;
```

The result is:

```
   SUM1      G_BUYER
17500.00     FX Properties Ltd
40000.00     Vista Estates Ltd
```

6.4 Further possibilities with joins

Joins can be a lot more complex than in the example shown above. So far, we have created joins from just two tables. In fact, it is quite possible to join three or even more tables together.

Furthermore, joins do not have to be based on the equals operator. All the examples that we have seen so far have been **equi-joins**. But a join can just as well be formed on the basis of other relational operators. We could, for instance, specify a join condition in which the values from column X had to be greater than those in column Y.

6.5 Subqueries

The SELECT command can be **nested**, as in the following example:
Query: When and for how much was 121 Wellington St. sold?

48

```
SELECT SaleDate, Price
FROM Sales
WHERE PropNum =
  (SELECT PropNum
  FROM Property
  WHERE HouseNum = '121'
  AND Street = 'Wellington St.');
```

Result:

SALEDATE	PRICE
25/02/80	25000
26/02/80	40000
27/02/80	50000

The SELECT command which appears in parentheses, that is:

```
(SELECT PropNum
FROM Property
WHERE HouseNum = '121'
AND Street = 'Wellington St.')
```

is known as the **inner** SELECT. In this example, the inner SELECT is evaluated first. Its job is to obtain the property number of the house at 121 Wellington Street.

dBASE IV/SQL then evaluates the **outer** SELECT, that is, the part of the command outside the parentheses. This makes use of the result produced by the inner SELECT.

The inner SELECT yields:

```
PROPNUM
1
```

The outer SELECT operates on this result. Once the inner SELECT has been evaluated, you can think of the entire command as being represented like this:

```
SELECT SaleDate, Price
FROM Sales
WHERE PropNum =
  1;
```

In this example, the inner SELECT must produce exactly one row.

If this was not the case, the comparison (in the outer SELECT) would be ambiguous. dBASE IV/SQL would then display the message 'Query did not return exactly one value'.

It is possible to construct queries in which the inner SELECT yields more than one row. However, you cannot do this if the outer SELECT uses the equals operator. In place of equals, you can use the IN predicate.

Query: Which properties were sold for more than £38,500?

```
SELECT HouseNum, Street
FROM Property
WHERE PropNum IN
  (SELECT PropNum
  FROM Sales
  WHERE Price > 38500);
```

Result:

HOUSENUM	STREET
121	Wellington St.
121	Wellington St.

The next example shows how several subqueries can be combined in a single command.

Query: Which properties were bought by either Vista or FX?

```
SELECT *
FROM Property
WHERE PropNum IN
  (SELECT PropNum
  FROM Sales
  WHERE Buyer = 'Vista Estates Ltd')
  OR PropNum IN
    (SELECT PropNum
    FROM Sales
    WHERE Buyer = 'FX Properties Ltd');
```

Result:

PROPNUM	HOUSENUM	STREET	YEARC	CONDITN
1	121	Wellington St.	1899	A
6	113	Wellington St.	1898	P
8	109	Wellington St.	1898	P

50

| 9 | 120 | Park Road | 1898 | P |
| 10 | 122 | Park Road | 1898 | G |

The above example is intended only to demonstrate the way in which more than one subquery can be incorporated into an SQL command. In fact, the command is more complex than necessary. The following version would serve just as well:

```
SELECT *
FROM Property
WHERE PropNum IN
   (SELECT PropNum
   FROM Sales
   WHERE Buyer = 'Vista Estates Ltd'
   OR Buyer = 'FX Properties Ltd');
```

Result:

PROPNUM	HOUSENUM	STREET	YEARC	CONDITN
1	121	Wellington St.	1899	A
6	113	Wellington St.	1898	P
8	109	Wellington St.	1898	P
9	120	Park Road	1898	P
10	122	Park Road	1898	G

Subqueries can exist at more than one **level** of nesting. Here is yet another version of the above command:

```
SELECT *
FROM Property
WHERE PropNum IN
   (SELECT PropNum
   FROM Sales
   WHERE Buyer = 'Vista Estates Ltd'
   OR PropNum IN
     (SELECT PropNum
     FROM Sales
     WHERE Buyer = 'FX Properties Ltd'));
```

Result:

PROPNUM	HOUSENUM	STREET	YEARC	CONDITN
1	121	Wellington St.	1899	A

6	113	Wellington St.	1898	P
8	109	Wellington St.	1898	P
9	120	Park Road	1898	P
10	122	Park Road	1898	G

6.6 The ANY predicate

By using the keyword ANY, we can test the WHERE condition against one or more values returned from the subquery.

Query: In which transactions was a price paid which was less than any of the prices paid by Vista Estates?

```
SELECT *
FROM Sales
WHERE Price < ANY
   (SELECT Price
   FROM Sales
   WHERE Buyer = 'Vista Estates Ltd');
```

Result:

PROP-NUM	SALE-DATE	PRICE	BUYER	SELLER
1	25/02/80	25000	FX Properties Ltd	P Johnson
6	01/12/81	22500	Vista Estates Ltd	T Taylor
3	11/11/81	17500	Ballerton D.C.	T Zander
8	01/01/82	20000	Vista Estates Ltd	L Lauder
9	30/01/82	30000	Vista Estates Ltd	W Bendix
10	05/05/83	35000	FX Properties Ltd	I Stevenson
10	22/05/83	37500	Vista Estates Ltd	FX Properties Ltd

The rows displayed by this query are those in which the price column has a value which is lower than the highest price paid by Vista Estates. The most that Vista paid for a property was £40,000. The result table therefore contains a row for each sale where the price was less than this figure.

The ANY predicate can use any of the relational operators.

6.7 The ALL predicate

The ALL keyword enables us to determine if the WHERE condition is true for every value returned from the subquery.

Query: In which transactions was a price paid which was less than all of the prices paid by Vista Estates?

```
SELECT *
FROM Sales
WHERE Price < ALL
  (SELECT Price
  FROM Sales
  WHERE Buyer = 'Vista Estates Ltd');
```

Result:

PROP-NUM	SALE-DATE	PRICE	BUYER	SELLER
3	11/11/81	17500	Ballerton D.C.	T Zander

6.8 The EXISTS predicate

When the EXISTS keyword is used with a subquery, the outer WHERE condition is true whenever the inner SELECT produces at least one row.

Query: Which properties have been sold one or more times?

```
SELECT HouseNum, Street
FROM Property
WHERE EXISTS
  (SELECT *
  FROM Sales
  WHERE Property.PropNum = Sales.PropNum);
```

Result:

HOUSENUM	STREET
121	Wellington St.
119	Wellington St.
113	Wellington St.
109	Wellington St.
120	Park Road
122	Park Road

The subquery returns true or false, depending on whether or not it produces any rows. When it returns true, the outer query is evaluated and a row is added to the result table.

The first row in the Property table has a PropNum of 1. In order for this row to be included in the result table, the subquery would have to yield at least one row, that is, there would have to be at least one row in the Sales table which also had a PropNum of 1. The Sales table does indeed have such a row so the first row of the Property table is placed in the result table. The second row of the Property table is evaluated in the same way, and so on.

It is also possible to reverse the selection, that is, to arrange for the outer SELECT to be evaluated only when the inner SELECT produces **no** rows. This is achieved with the NOT EXISTS predicate.

Query: Which properties have never been sold?

```
SELECT HouseNum, Street
FROM Property
WHERE NOT EXISTS
  (SELECT *
  FROM Sales
  WHERE Property.PropNum = Sales.PropNum);
```

Result:

HOUSENUM	STREET
123	Wellington St.
117	Wellington St.
115	Wellington St.
111	Wellington St.

6.9 Correlated subqueries

In all of the subqueries which we have looked at so far (except those involving EXISTS), each of the SELECTs is evaluated in turn. First, the inner SELECT is evaluated – in full, once only. Then the outer SELECT is evaluated. These types of queries are called **simple subqueries**.

By contrast, in a **correlated subquery**, the inner SELECT is evaluated many times. To be exact, it is evaluated once for each row in the outer SELECT. On each evaluation, it uses values which the outer SELECT supplies to it.

Because the inner and outer SELECTs use the same rows at the same time, you must use table aliases to distinguish them (see Section 6.3 for a discussion on table aliases).

The following example demonstrates a correlated subquery.

Query: Find the most expensive property pruchased by each buyer.

```
SELECT outer.PropNum, outer.Price, outer.Buyer
FROM Sales outer
WHERE Price =
  (SELECT MAX(Price)
  FROM Sales inner
  WHERE outer.Buyer = inner.Buyer);
```

Result:

outer->PropNum	outer->Price	outer->Buyer
1	40000	Vista Estates Ltd
1	50000	Ballerton D.C.
10	35000	FX Properties Ltd

In this example, each row which the outer SELECT evaluates causes the inner SELECT to be executed. The inner SELECT takes the buyer from this row, and searches the Sales table for the highest price which that buyer has paid. This price is then used by the outer SELECT to determine whether the row should be sent to the result table.

6.10 Combining the results of two or more SELECTs

By using the keyword UNION, you can join together the result tables from several separate SELECTs. In doing so, any duplicate rows are automatically filtered out.

Two conditions are necessary in order for this to work: each of the result tables must have the same number of columns; and the columns must match in their data types and widths.

In the next example, a single result table is created. This has one column which contains all the values from the buyer and seller columns, with duplicates being eliminated.

```
SELECT Buyer
FROM Sales UNION
SELECT Seller
FROM Sales;
```

The single result table is:

```
BUYER
W Bendix
FX Properties Ltd
```

Ballerton D.C.
P Johnson
L Lauder
I Stevenson
Vista Estates Ltd
T Taylor
T Zander

6.11 Storing a query result in a new table

You can temporarily store the results of a SELECT command in a new table. This table can then be used in turn with other SQL commands. In order to create a new table in this way, add the following clause to the SELECT:

```
SAVE TO TEMP table name
```

Query: Create a temporary table containing all the properties in poor condition, and name this table Slums.

```
SELECT *
FROM Property
WHERE Conditn = 'P'
SAVE TO TEMP Slums;
```

Now let's check that it has worked.

```
SELECT *
FROM Slums;
```

The result it:

PROPNUM	HOUSENUM	STREET	YEARC	CONDITN
5	115	Wellington St.	1899	P
6	113	Wellington St.	1898	P
7	111	Wellington St.	1898	P
8	109	Wellington St.	1898	P
9	120	Park Road	1898	P

When you exit from SQL, the temporary table will disappear. In order to retain the temporary table, you add the keyword KEEP to the SAVE TO clause. So to retain the Slums table, you would issue the following command:

```
SELECT *
FROM Property
WHERE Conditn = "P"
SAVE TO TEMP Slums KEEP;
```

Although this command stores the slum data in a file, this is still not a permanent part of the SQL database. If, after exiting from SQL, you examined the Housing sub-directory, you would see a file named SLUMS.DBF there. But there is no record of this file in the catalogue tables. The next time that you go into SQL, you will not be able to access the table as part of the database.

This can be overcome by issuing the following command:

```
DBDEFINE Slums;
```

This causes the catalogue tables to be updated with information about the slums table (of course, you must start the Housing database first).

The DBDEFINE command cannot be issued in the same SQL session in which the table was created.

6.11.1 Column names in temporary tables

A list of column names can be included in the SAVE TO TEMP clause. This list is mandatory if any of the columns is generated by an aggregate function or contains a calculated field.

The next example creates a file named SUMMARY.DBF, containing a record for each buyer. The record contains the buyer's name and the number of properties which the buyer has bought.

```
SELECT Buyer, COUNT(Buyer)
FROM Sales
GROUP BY Buyer
SAVE TO TEMP summary (Buyer, Number) KEEP;
```

6.12 Syntax diagram for the SELECT command

A **syntax diagram** is often used to summarise the clauses and options in a particular command. A syntax diagram provides a concise and exact definition of a command, but it offers nothing in the way of explanation. The best way of using it is in conjunction with a set of examples which illustrate the workings of the command.

Syntax diagrams, as they appear in manuals and on dBASE IV/SQL help screens, use the notation indicated in Table 6.1.

Table 6.1. Notation used in syntax diagrams

Symbol	Meaning
< >	Text appearing between angle brackets represents an item which the user must supply.
[ ]	Anything appearing between square brackets is optional.
/	Where a slash separates items in a list, just one of the items must be selected.
[...]	A series of dots means that the preceding item may be repeated an indefinite number of times.

The syntax diagram for the SELECT command is:

```
<SELECT clause>
[<INTO clause>]
<FROM clause>
[<WHERE clause>]
[<GROUP BY clause> [<HAVING clause>]]
[<UNION subquery>] ...
[<ORDER BY clause> / <FOR UPDATE OF clause>]
[<SAVE TO TEMP clause>]
```

This is read as follows. The SELECT command begins with a mandatory SELECT clause, followed by an optional INTO clause (we will examine the INTO clause in Chapter 11).

Next comes a mandatory FROM clause and an optional WHERE clause. This is followed by an optional GROUP BY clause. If, and only if, the GROUP BY clause is present, an optional HAVING clause may be used.

Next, there is either an ORDER BY or a FOR UPDATE clause. They are both optional, but since they are separated by a slash, you can use either one or the other – not both at the same time (we shall come back to the FOR UPDATE clause in Chapter 11). The command may be terminated with a SAVE TO TEMP clause. Finally, the command may include the word UNION, followed by another complete SELECT command.

6.13 An introduction to catalogues

An SQL database does not only hold the tables which you create yourself. Each database also has a set of 10 **catalogue tables**. SQL uses these tables for housekeeping purposes, and to help it to deal with queries in an efficient manner.

58

An introduction to catalogues

You can use the catalogue tables to obtain information about the database itself. The most important of the tables, called Syscols, contains details of all the columns in all the tables in the database (including the catalogue tables). Given that you generally need the exact names of the columns and tables – and perhaps data types and field lengths – in order to do anything useful with the database, the following query is likely to be one that you will use frequently:

Query: What are the names of all the tables in my database? What are the names, lengths and data types of the columns in each table?

```
SELECT Colname, ColType, ColLen, TBName
FROM Syscols
WHERE NOT TBName LIKE 'SYS%';
```

This query takes advantage of the fact that the names of all ten catalogue tables begin with SYS. By excluding tables which match SYS in their first three letters, we can filter out the catalogues themselves from the result, thereby allowing us to concentrate on the tables which contain actual data.

In our example database, the above query would generate the following result table:

COLNAME	COLTYPE	COLLEN	TBNAME
PROPNUM	N	11	PROPERTY
HOUSENUM	C	6	PROPERTY
STREET	C	20	PROPERTY
YEARC	N	6	PROPERTY
CONDITN	C	1	PROPERTY
PROPNUM	N	11	SALES
SALEDATE	D	8	SALES
PRICE	N	11	SALES
BUYER	C	20	SALES
SELLER	C	20	SALES
H_TYPE	C	8	HELPTAB
H_NUMBER	N	11	HELPTAB

This shows us the name of each column, then the type of the column, its length, and the name of the table which holds the column.

Note that the type indicated for YearC and Price are both N. These columns were defined as SMALLINT and INTEGER respectively. They are, however, both numeric types, and as such are interchangeable with all other numeric types (including NUMERIC, DECIMAL and FLOAT).

CHAPTER SEVEN

Maintaining the database

In this chapter, we will deal with various methods of keeping the database up to date, including altering and deleting rows, deleting entire tables and databases, altering the structure of a table, and creating indexes

7.1 Altering rows

As well as allowing us to do searches, SQL can be used to change the data in a table. The following SQL command changes the condition field of all properties in Park Road to 'Good':

```
UPDATE Property SET Conditn = 'G'
WHERE Street = 'Park Road';
```

The computer replies:

```
2 row(s) updated
```

7.2 Deleting rows

The following command can be used to delete rows from a table:

```
DELETE FROM table name
WHERE condition;
```

The WHERE clause includes a condition which specifies which rows are to be deleted. This condition is formed in exactly the same way as in the SELECT command.

If the WHERE clause is omitted, the entire table will be cleared.

7.3 Deleting an entire table

The following command will remove an entire table from the database:

```
DROP TABLE table name;
```

7.4 Erasing the database

This command permanently removes the database from the system:

```
DROP DATABASE database name;
```

7.5 Altering the structure of a table

Suppose that we wanted to extend the property table by adding two columns. The first would indicate the type of property, for example, 'residential only' or 'mixed residential and business'. The second would show the size of the building.

You can extend a table in this way by using the ALTER TABLE command:

```
ALTER TABLE Property
ADD (PropType CHAR(20), Size SMALLINT);
```

This command adds the two specified columns to the table.

ALTER TABLE is the only SQL command which can be used to modify the structure of a table directly. If you wanted to do more than just add columns to the table, you would have to take a roundabout route. You would have to store the data from the table in a temporary file, delete the table, create a new table with the modified structure, and transfer the data from the temporary file to the new table.

Suppose that we decided to increase the lengths of the Buyer and Seller columns in the Sales table to 22 characters. The steps needed to achieve this would be as follows:

```
START DATABASE Housing;
UNLOAD DATA TO tempfile.dbf
FROM TABLE Sales;
```

The UNLOAD DATA command creates a new data file (that is, a .DBF file) and copies the data to it. In this case, the name of the file

61

is Tempfile.Dbf.

```
DROP TABLE Sales;
```

This command deletes the Sales table.
Next, we must re-create the Sales table with a new structure:

```
CREATE TABLE Sales
(PropNum INTEGER, SaleDate DATE,
Price INTEGER, Buyer CHAR(22),
Seller CHAR(22));
```

In this new structure, the columns for Buyer and Seller have been increased in size. The data from the temporary file, Tempfile.Dbf, can now be copied back to the table:

```
LOAD DATA FROM tempfile.dbf
INTO TABLE Sales;
```

Finally, we delete the temporary file:

```
ERASE tempfile.dbf
```

7.6 Indexing

If a table has a large number of records, searching can be very sluggish. In order to execute a SELECT query, the computer has to retrieve each record in turn from the disk and test it against the search criterion. One way of speeding up this process is to create **index tables** for some or all columns.

This sort of index is analogous to the index that you find at the back of a book. It is a list of key values – words, numbers, dates – with an indication of the records in which each value occurs. Like the index in a book, the list is stored in a particular sequence: alphabetical, numerical or chronological, ascending or descending. Searching with an index is fast because the computer no longer has to retrieve the entire table in order to find the required records.

Index tables are created by means of the CREATE INDEX command. This command can create indexes for several columns at the same time. For each column, the command can specify either ascending or descending sequence.

The following command indexes the Sales table on property number and seller:

62

```
CREATE INDEX SaleIndx
ON Sales (PropNum, Seller);
```

Each index must have a name. In this example, the name is SaleIndx.

In order to create an index in descending order, the keyword DESC must be placed after the relevant column name. You cannot mix ascending and descending columns in the same index. To create a descending index on property number, the following command could be issued:

```
CREATE INDEX PropNumx
ON Sales (PropNum DESC);
```

It is not possible to index on a column whose type is LOGICAL.

Clearly, index tables have to be kept up to date. When you add or amend rows in the table, the index has to be updated to reflect the changes. Fortunately, SQL handles this automatically. However, the updating of indexes takes time, and can therefore slow down the updating of the table. For this reason, it is a good idea only to index the columns which you are fairly sure will be used in searches.

The SysIdxs catalogue table contains information about the indexes which exist in the database.

7.6.1 Indexes with unique keys

In the Property table, the PropNum column contains unique values, that is, no property number ever occurs more than once in the table. At least, that is the intention. But it is possible that somebody will accidently input a record which is already present in the table, or that a new property number will be issued which is the same as that of an existing property.

This sort of mistake can be avoided by using the UNIQUE option when creating indexes. Once you have done this, dBASE IV/SQL will no longer allow rows with duplicate keys to be input.

The UNIQUE option is specified as follows:

```
CREATE UNIQUE INDEX PropUnq
ON Property (PropNum);
```

Be aware that the time needed to update a unique index is slightly more than with an ordinary index.

CHAPTER EIGHT

Full-screen working

8.1 Introduction

In many respects, SQL is a far more powerful programming language than the one built into dBASE IV. But it lacks any facilities for **full-screen working**, that is, for creating data-entry forms, menus, and other interactive devices aimed at making life easier for the non-technical user.

dBASE IV, by contrast, is a highly interactive system. It provides many ways of 'hiding' the technicalities of data management from end users. For example, it provides easy methods for browsing and editing tables, for setting up new tables, for performing searches and for selecting from menus. The end user can employ these features in an intuitive manner, without needing to learn any complex syntax, and often without having to know the names of the columns and table in the database.

If you decide to use SQL as your main programming language within dBASE IV, you do not have to give up the idea of full-screen working. Many of dBASE IV's interactive commands can also be used with SQL databases, independently of SQL. They include the following:

(a) BROWSE (for browsing and editing a table in tabular format);

(b) EDIT (for browsing and editing a table one record at a time);

(c) APPEND (for adding new records);

(d) CREATE (for creating new tables).

8.2 Working outside SQL

As far as the SQL user is concerned, a database is simply a collection of tables. You have to know its name and the names of the tables which it contains. But you do not need to worry about the physical structure of data on the disk, the names of the files which hold the database, or the directories in which those files reside.

SQL itself has access to all the information it needs about files and directories. In particular, it knows which SQL databases exist, which tables are in them, and where they are located within the directory structure of the disk. It obtains these details from the catalogue tables, and also from a special database called SQLHOME.

However, in order to access a database when working **outside** SQL, the user does need to know about the files and directories in which it is stored. In particular, you should be aware of the following points:

(a) An SQL database is a DOS sub-directory, the name of which is the same as the name of the database.

(b) Each table within the database is a separate data file; the name of this file is the same as the table name, but with the suffix .DBF.

Our sample Housing database would therefore be a sub-directory with a name such as C:\DBASE\HOUSING. The contents of the directory **path** (in this case, C:\DBASE\) depends on where you happened to be within the directory structure when the database was created.

In the same example, the Property table would be a file with the name C:\DBASE\HOUSING\PROPERTY.DBF.

If you want to work with an SQL table from outside SQL, you need to know exactly where the table is located within the directory structure. To find this out, issue the following SQL command:

```
SHOW DATABASE;
```

The output from this command looks something like this:

```
Existing databases are:
```

NAME	CREATOR	CREATED	PATH
HOUSING		20/01/92	C:\DBASE\HOUSING

This tells us that there is one database, named Housing, and that its tables reside in the C:\DBASE\HOUSING directory.

In order to access a data file (that is, a table) from within the dBASE IV language (as opposed to SQL), the file must first be opened. This is accomplished with the following command:

65

```
USE datafile name
```

For example, if you wanted to work with the property table from the Housing database while outside SQL, you would issue this command:

```
USE C:\DBASE\HOUSING\PROPERTY
```

The USE command requires the entire path (or the path relative to the current directory). If the SHOW DATABASE command gave the path of the Housing database as, say, C:\PCLAB\DEMO\HOUSING, then the USE command for the property table would be:

```
USE C:\PCLAB\DEMO\HOUSING\PROPERTY
```

8.3 Browsing and editing an SQL database

Once the table has been opened by means of the USE command, it is possible to browse and edit it. The relevant dBASE IV commands are BROWSE and EDIT respectively. In fact, both commands allow you to browse through the table, and both allow you to edit the data. They vary only in the ways in which they display information on the screen.

When you issue the BROWSE command, dBASE IV displays a Browse screen (see Fig. 8.1). This shows the table in a tabular

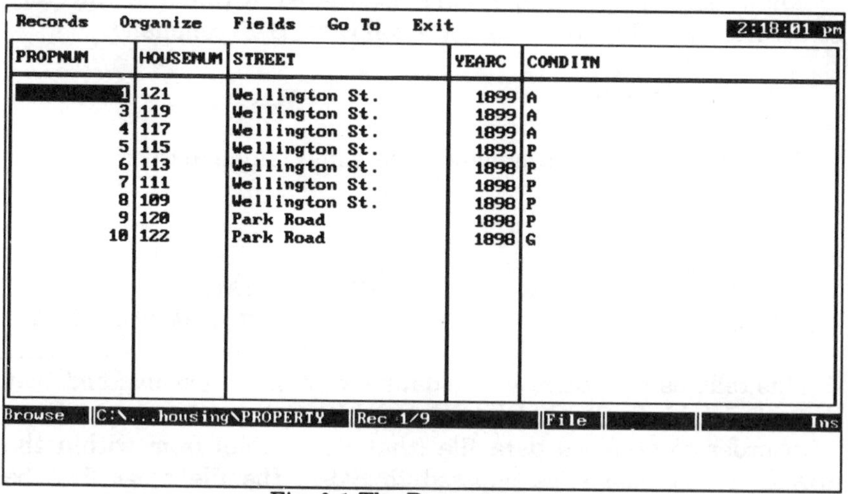

PROPNUM	HOUSENUM	STREET	YEARC	CONDITN
1	121	Wellington St.	1899	A
3	119	Wellington St.	1899	A
4	117	Wellington St.	1899	A
5	115	Wellington St.	1899	P
6	113	Wellington St.	1898	P
7	111	Wellington St.	1898	P
8	109	Wellington St.	1898	P
9	120	Park Road	1898	P
10	122	Park Road	1898	G

Records   Organize   Fields   Go To   Exit   2:18:01 pm

Browse   C:\...housing\PROPERTY   Rec 1/9   File   Ins

Fig. 8.1 The Browse screen.

66

format, with one record (row) of the table occupying one row on the screen.

Pressing the TAB key within the Browse screen causes the cursor to move one column to the right. To move the cursor one column to the left, press Shift-TAB. The up and down arrow keys, and the PgUp and PgDn keys, move the cursor vertically, one row or 'page' at a time. If there are more rows in the table than will fit on the screen, these keys will allow you to scroll vertically through the table. To edit the data, simply move the cursor to the relevant field and overtype the old data.

If you pass the cursor downwards through the last row in the table, dBASE IV asks you if you wish to add new records to the file.

The f10 key opens a menu at the top of the Browse screen. Among other things, this menu allows you to search for values in the column which currently holds the cursor.

The EDIT command displays a table in Edit format, that is, with one record occupying the entire screen (see Fig. 8.2).

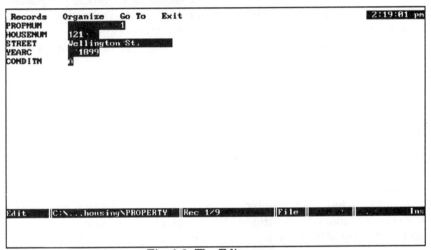

Fig. 8.2 The Edit screen.

To change the data in the record which is currently on the screen, you move the cursor to the relevant field (press Enter to move down one field) and overtype the old text. When you pass the cursor through the final field in the record, the next record in the table will be displayed. Pressing PgDn and PgUp enables you to browse forwards and backwards through adjacent records.

By pressing the f2 key, you can switch from Browse mode (tabular format) to Edit mode (one record at a time), and vice versa.

There are two ways of exiting the Browse and Edit screens:

(a) Press Ctrl-End. This causes all amended records to be written to the file. Any changes to the data become definite.

(b) Press ESC. This also causes amended records to be written to the file, except that any changes made since the cursor entered the current record will be discarded.

If you only want to add new records to the table, issue the command:

```
APPEND
```

The f2 key is available in Append mode for switching between the two ways of viewing the data (tabular and record-by-record). Press Ctrl-End to exit Append mode and write the new data to disk.

As we have already seen, dBASE IV/SQL maintains important information in the catalogue tables. One of the functions of this information is to help the system to execute SQL commands efficiently. However, this information is not automatically updated when you use APPEND to add new data to a table. Instead, you must update it explicitly. To do so, run the following SQL command whenever you have added a reasonable amount of new data to a database:

```
RUNSTATS;
```

8.4 Creating tables in full-screen mode

In Chapter 4, we saw how to use the SQL command CREATE TABLE to set up a new table. You can also set up tables interactively, from outside SQL.

Suppose that you wanted to build up a database containing information about corporations. A convenient way of doing this would be to start by setting up an empty database, using a command such as:

```
CREATE DATABASE Corps;
```

The effect of this would be to create a new, empty directory called CORPS. The full path to this directory would depend on which directory was current at the time that the CREATE DATABASE command was issued. (It is also possible to define a full path name explicitly with CREATE DATABASE.)

Having issued the CREATE DATABASE command, you can use

SHOW DATABASE to determine the full path of the sub-directory which you just created. SHOW DATABASE would display something similar to the following:

```
Existing databases are:
```

NAME	CREATOR	CREATED	PATH
HOUSING		20/01/92	C:\DBASE\HOUSING
CORPS		10/02/92	C:\TEST\CORPS

The next step is to create a table in the C:\TEST\CORPS sub-directory. This is achieved with the following dBASE IV command:

```
CREATE firms.dbf
```

Unlike BROWSE, EDIT and APPEND, this form of the CREATE command cannot be issued from the SQL. prompt. To use the command, you must first leave SQL **mode**.

dBASE IV can be used in two distinct modes: SQL mode and dBASE mode. In the previous chapters, we were working entirely in SQL mode. In this mode (which is characterised by the SQL. prompt), any SQL command may be issued, along with a restricted repertoire of dBASE commands. These include MODIFY FILE and QUIT. SQL mode does not allow the use of dBASE commands which manipulate data in tables, with the exceptions of BROWSE, EDIT and APPEND.

In dBASE mode (which is characterised by the dot prompt), all dBASE commands are permitted, but no SQL commands are allowed.

You switch from dBASE mode to SQL mode by means of the following command:

```
SET SQL ON
```

To go back to dBASE mode, you type:

```
SET SQL OFF
```

In order to create a table interactively, you must therefore first exit SQL. You then issue a CREATE command (for example, for a file named Firms), as follows:

```
CREATE \test\corps\firms
```

dBASE IV responds by displaying the Create screen, as shown in Fig. 8.3. You use this screen to enter the details of the columns

69

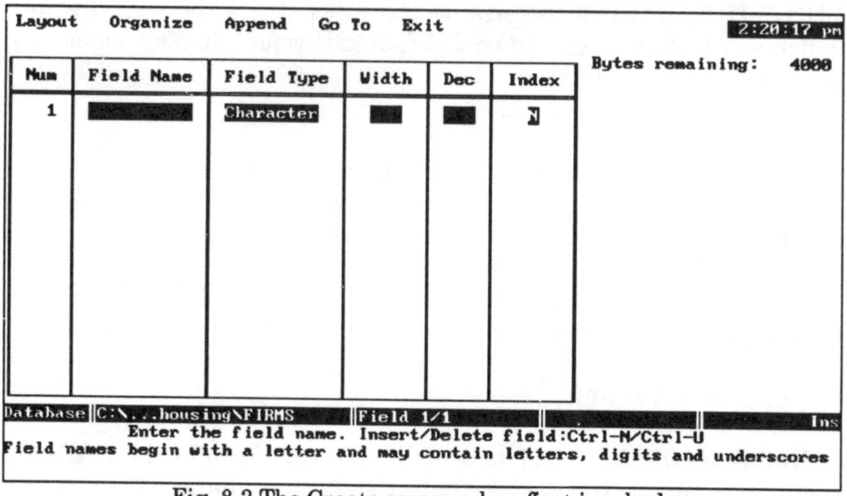

Layout	Organize	Append	Go To	Exit			2:20:17 pm

Bytes remaining: 4000

Num	Field Name	Field Type	Width	Dec	Index
1	▓▓▓▓▓▓	Character	▓▓	▓▓	N

Database C:\...housing\FIRMS   Field 1/1   Ins
        Enter the field name. Insert/Delete field:Ctrl-N/Ctrl-U
Field names begin with a letter and may contain letters, digits and underscores

Fig. 8.3 The Create screen when first invoked.

(fields) in the table which you are creating. In the case of the field type, you can use the space bar to help choose between the various options. Each time that you press the space bar, another data type is displayed.

When you have finished entering the details of your new table, the screen will appear as in Fig. 8.4.

When you press Ctrl-End from inside the Create screen, dBASE IV

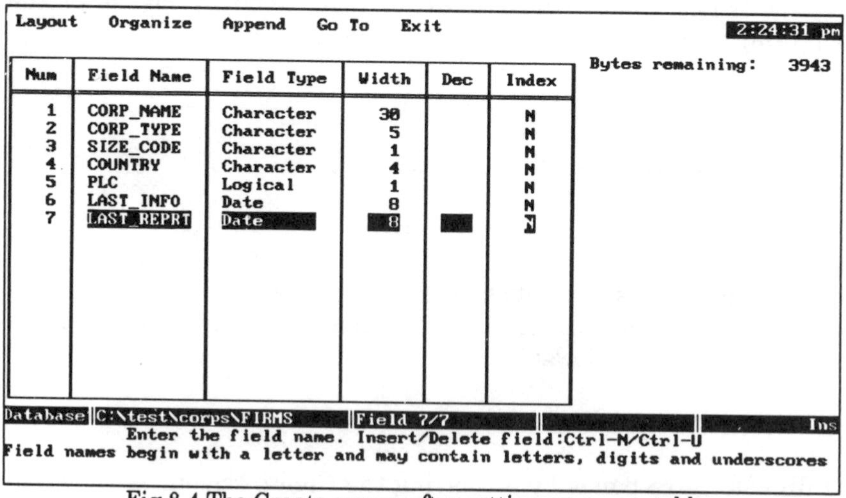

Layout	Organize	Append	Go To	Exit			2:24:31 pm

Bytes remaining: 3943

Num	Field Name	Field Type	Width	Dec	Index
1	CORP_NAME	Character	30		N
2	CORP_TYPE	Character	5		N
3	SIZE_CODE	Character	1		N
4	COUNTRY	Character	4		N
5	PLC	Logical	1		N
6	LAST_INFO	Date	8		N
7	LAST_REPRT	Date	8	▓▓	N

Database C:\test\corps\FIRMS   Field 7/7   Ins
        Enter the field name. Insert/Delete field:Ctrl-N/Ctrl-U
Field names begin with a letter and may contain letters, digits and underscores

Fig 8.4 The Create screen after setting up a new table.

goes ahead and creates the table. It will then ask you if you want to enter new records straight away.

What we now have is a directory called CORP. In this directory, there is a data file named Firms.Dbf, as well as a number of empty catalogue tables. The data file will be used as one of the tables in the SQL database.

However, there is still something missing. Although the catalogue tables exist, they do not yet contain any details of the columns within the Firms table.

To rectify this, first close the Firms.Dbf file. This is accomplished with the following dBASE command:

```
CLOSE DATABASES
```

(This can be abbreviated to CLOS DATA.) Next, go back to SQL mode:

```
SET SQL ON
```

and issue this SQL command:

```
DBDEFINE;
```

dBASE IV/SQL will look in the sub-directory for any tables for which no information has yet been stored in the catalogue tables. It then updates the catalogues, and replies as follows:

```
Table(s) DBDEFINEd
FIRMS

DBDEFINE successful
```

If the database contains several different tables, you create each one individually with a separate CREATE command. However, you can add them to the SQL database *en bloc* by issuing DBDEFINE just once.

If you use the dBASE CREATE command to create a file for an SQL database which already holds some tables, you must, as part of the DBDEFINE command, specify the actual name of the table which you are adding to the database, for example:

```
DBDEFINE Firms;
```

71

CHAPTER NINE

Database design

9.1 Introduction

In this chapter, we will examine some of the factors which govern the design of a database. In particular, we will look at ways of deciding how the data should be organised among the various tables, which columns the tables should contain, and how those columns should be linked. This process is sometimes called **data modelling**.

The chapter begins with the concept of **integrity**. This is one of the important goals of database design. We will discuss a number of common-sense rules which help bring the goal closer. We will also take an introductory look at **normalisation theory**, which is essentially a formalisation of the same common-sense rules.

A database does not only need a good logical structure. It must also be an adequate model of some aspect of the real world. Two diagrammatic techniques are often used to help ensure that the database is a realistic model. They are called **data-flow diagrams** and **entity/relationship diagrams**. We will close the chapter with an illustration of these techniques.

Although this chapter concentrates on the structure of the database, the overall design process also covers several other steps, typically: analysing information requirements and data flow; drawing up specifications; and building a prototype.

9.2 Integrity

Many people, when setting up a database, tend to go about things in a more-or-less intuitive way. Although this can produce perfectly satisfactory results, it could also lead to problems. It is important to understand what these problems are in order to avoid them.

A poor design can result in data which is impossible to retrieve. Furthermore, the deletion of some data could inadvertently lead to the deletion of other data. A poor design can also contribute to inconsistencies. These can occur when the same item of data is stored in different places. For example, if a person's address is duplicated in the database, and if the person moves home, each instance of the address would have to be amended. This leads to the possibility of the database having different addresses for the same person. The result: you can no longer rely on the accuracy of the address data.

This concern with **integrity** is an important aspect of good database design. A well-designed database is one for which it is relatively easy to formulate queries. Good design also leads to databases which are easily extendible.

We can identify several rules of thumb which can help to ensure that the database has a good design

Rule 1: **Every table must have a primary key**

A primary key is a field which serves as a unique identification for the records in the table. It does not have to be a single field: it could be formed from a combination of fields. But it must contain a different value for every row in the table. This implies that the rows themselves contain unique data: that each row represents a different instance of whatever 'thing' the table is concerned with.

In the Property table, the primary key is obvious: it is the property number (PropNum). Each property appears in the table once only, and each has a different property number. If property numbers did not exist, the property's address (that is, the combination of its house number and street) could serve as a primary key, since different houses cannot have the same address.

In the Sales table, the primary key is not so obvious. The property number would not be suitable because it is not unique within the table. The same property can be sold any number of times. Nor could the combination of property number and date of sale be used, since a given property could be sold more than once on the same day. And who is to say that the same property could not be sold more than once on the same day and at the same price? So even the combination of property number, date and price could not serve as a guaranteed unique identification for each row.

Property number, date, price and buyer could together form a unique identification. Even if the same property was sold twice on the same day at the same price, it would not then be bought again by the original buyer at that price and on that date. Similarly, property number, date, price and seller could serve as a unique identification. The sales table therefore has two possible primary keys.

Rule 2: **Make each entity into a separate table**

An **entity** is a basic object which is represented in the database. A property is one example of an entity; a sale is another. Each entity should be the subject of its own table.

Each entity has a number of distinct characteristics, and these characteristics form the attributes of the table. A property is characterised by its house number, street name, year of construction and structural condition. These characteristics are therefore the attributes of the Property table. Similarly, the characteristics of a sale are its date, price, name of buyer and name of seller. Why not include house number and street among the characteristics of a sale? Because each characteristic must be assigned to the entity to which it is most appropriate.

A good way of illustrating the importance of these rules is to look at some examples of databases in which the rules have been ignored. (This method of explanation is derived from C.J. Date (1983), p. 207.)

In the first example, all the data is placed in one table. The table has a single record for each property, with the following columns:

Property number
House number
Street
Year
Condition
Sale Date 1
Price 1
Buyer 1
Seller 1
Sale Date 2
Price 2
Buyer 2
Seller 2
Sale Date 3
Price 3
Buyer 3
Seller 3

This design has some serious drawbacks. Firstly, there is an artificial limit on the number of times a property can be sold. The database is supposed to be a model of the real world , but it fails to take account of the possibility of a property being sold more than three times. Conversely, for properties which are sold fewer than three times, there is considerable waste of space within the table.

Another problem is that some searches would be extremely laborious. Imagine that you wanted to know which properties had been sold by Vista Estates. The only way to find out would be through a very long-winded command, such as:

```
SELECT HouseNum, Street
FROM Property
WHERE Buyer_1 = 'Vista Estates Ltd'
OR Buyer_2 = 'Vista Estates Ltd'
OR Buyer_3 = 'Vista Estates Ltd';
```

A final, less important, objection is that the table would be very wide, so the data would not all fit across the width of the screen.

In the second example, there is also just one table for the entire data, but here the table contains one record for each sale. The columns are:

> Sale date
> Property number
> House number
> Street
> Condition
> Year
> Price
> Buyer
> Seller

The main disadvantage of this design is **redundancy**. A given property can be sold many times, but each sales record must hold the same basic data about the property itself (house number, street, condition, etc.). Not only does this involve additional typing, it means that there is a risk of inconsistencies creeping into the data. If it became necessary to change the structural condition of a given property, the same change would have to be made to every row containing details of that property. If, in doing so, the user made a mistake, that item of data would no longer be reliable.

9.3 One-to-many relationships

The third rule of thumb is concerned with the ways in which tables are linked together. Before discussing this rule, we must first clarify some terminology.

Our sample database consists of two tables. These tables are linked according to the contents of the PropNum field in the Property table and the PropNum field in the Sales table (see Fig. 9.1).

Property Table (One)

PropNum PRIMARY KEY	HouseNum	Street	YearC	Conditn

Sales Table (Many)

PropNum FOREIGN KEY	SaleDate	Price	Buyer	Seller

Fig. 9.1 The sample database, showing how the tables are linked.

This type of linkage is called a **one-to-many relationship**. In this case, the Property table is the 'one'-table because each PropNum in this table occurs just once (otherwise it could not be a primary key). The Sales table is the 'many'-table because the same property number can occur any number of times in the table.

Each possible value for PropNum in the Sales table must also exist in the Property table. This implies that a sale cannot be recorded for a property until the details of that property have been entered into the Property table.

When an attribute in one table (in this case, Sales) depends in this way on the primary key of another table (in this case, Property), that attribute is called a **foreign key**. In Fig. 9.1, the single-headed arrow indicates the primary key and a double-headed arrow indicates the foreign key.

The third rule can therefore be expressed as follows:

Rule 3: **In a one-to-many relationship, the tables are linked by means of the primary key in the 'one'-table and a foreign key in the 'many'-table.**

This aspect of the database design is called **referential integrity**.

9.4 Many-to-many relationships

As well as one-to-many relationships (and one-to-one relationships), it is possible to have **many-to-many relationships**.

Suppose that we decided to add a table containing data about the people who own the properties. The table might show the people's addresses and phone numbers, perhaps. It is possible that some properties are owned by more than one person – for example, a group of co-owners – and also that a given owner might own other properties. The link between properties and owners is therefore a **many-to-many relationship**.

A many-to-many relationship can be thought of a combination of two one-to-many relationships. In order to represent it in the database, it is necessary to add an additional table. In our example database, the entity in this additional table would be 'ownerships' (see Fig. 9.2).

The many-to-many relationship between properties and owners is therefore made up of:

(a) a one-to-many relationship between properties and ownerships; and

(b) a one-to-many relationship between ownerships and owners.

The rule of thumb for one-to-many relationships – that the tables must be linked by means of the primary key in the 'one'-table and a foreign key in the 'many'-table – applies equally here, as shown in Fig. 9.3.

In the theoretical literature on database design, the term **normalisation** is used to describe the process of designing tables in such a way as to promote integrity. There exists a hierarchy of five **normal forms**. The higher the normal form, the closer the design approaches the ideal. If the rules given in this chapter are followed, the database is said to be in the **third normal form**. This is adequate for most practical purposes.

9.5 Normalisation theory (This section can be skipped on a first reading.)

In this section, we will make use of a new example: a database of books in a library. The design of the database is influenced by a number of factors:

(a) A book can have more than one author.

(b) Each book is allocated to a single subject category.

Property Table (One)

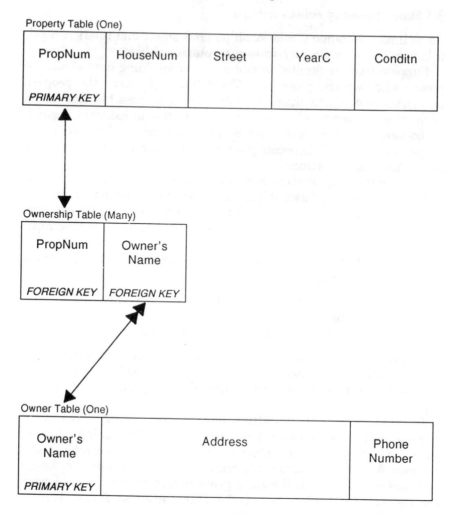

PropNum	HouseNum	Street	YearC	Conditn
PRIMARY KEY				

Ownership Table (Many)

PropNum	Owner's Name
FOREIGN KEY	*FOREIGN KEY*

Owner Table (One)

Owner's Name	Address	Phone Number
PRIMARY KEY		

Fig. 9.2 A many-to-many relationship with an additional table.

(c)   For each subject, it is required to keep a record of the number of titles in stock.

We will use the following sample tables, linked together as shown in Fig. 9.3.

```
Book table
BOOKNUM      TITLE                    SUBJECT
1            Five minute dBASE        Computing
```

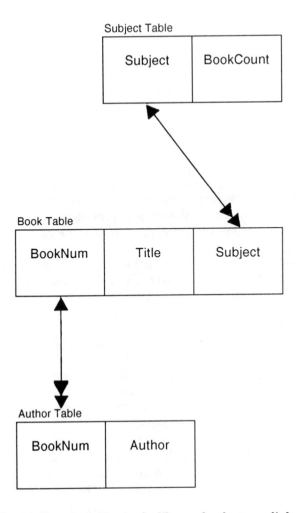

Fig. 9.3 How the tables in the library database are linked.

2	SQL explained	Computing
3	More dBASE	Computing
4	How to sell	Marketing

```
Subject table
SUBJECT    BOOKCOUNT
Computing  3
Marketing  1
```

```
Author table
BOOKNUM    AUTHOR
1          Bill Garth
2          Philip Klein
3          Mike la Salle
3          Hans Pietersen
4          John Scarman
```

This design is sound. Although some obvious alternative designs are possible, these would involve fewer tables and therefore a higher degree of redundancy and a greater risk of inconsistency.

Normalisation theory helps us to understand the reasons that one relational database design is intrinsically better than another. This theory is essentially a formal way of expressing the simple common sense rules that we have discussed, such as the reasons for avoiding redundancy.

Normalisation theory presents a hierarchy of normal forms. The higher the normal form, the closer it is to the ideal logical database structure. The designs we have considered so far represent the third normal form, which is generally considered adequate for most purposes.

In theoretical database literature, the word **relation** is generally used rather than 'table'. A relation in this context is the expression of the way in which a number of groups of objects are associated. Thus, the Property table expresses the association between groups of property numbers, house numbers, street names, etc. The words 'relation' and 'table' are interchangeable.

A relation is said to be in the first normal form if it only has **atomic** values, that is, if no field contains more than one instance of the field's data. The following relation would not be in the first normal form because the third row contains two instances of authors.

```
Author table
BOOKNUM    AUTHOR
1          Bill Garth
2          Philip Klein
3          Mike la Salle; Hans Pietersen
4          John Scarman
```

All the examples of relations which we saw in Sections 9.2 to 9.4, including the 'bad' examples, are in the first normal form. The following example, which introduces some redundancy into the library database, is also of the first normal form:

BOOK-NUM	TITLE	AUTHOR	SUBJECT	BK-COUNT
1	Five minute dBASE	Bill Garth	Computing	3
2	SQL explained	Philip Klein	Computing	3
3	More dBASE	Mike la Salle	Computing	3
3	More dBASE	Hans Pietersen	Computing	3
4	How to sell	John Scarman	Marketing	1

Before looking at the second and third normal forms, we must discuss a new concept: **functional dependency**. Attribute Y is said to be functionally dependent on attribute X if there is exactly one value of Y for each value of X. This means that, if we know the value of X, it is possible to determine the value of Y – though the opposite is not necessarily the case.

In the present example, the subject category is functionally dependent on the book number because each book belongs to exactly one subject. Conversely, book number is not functionally dependent on subject, since any one subject contains an arbitrary number of books.

The author attribute is not functionally dependent on book number since a given book number can have more than one author. Title is functionally dependent on book number – each title corresponds to one number. But is book number functionally dependent on title? That depends on whether we assume that two different books can have exactly the same title. Functional dependency is thus often a matter of semantics.

We can now arrive at a definition of the second normal form. A table is in the second normal form if:

(a)   the table is in the first normal form; and
(b)   every attribute in the table which is not an element of the primary key is functionally dependent on the primary key.

(As we saw earlier, a table's primary key can be made up of a combination of attributes. Where this is the case, functional dependency represents **complete** dependency, not merely dependency on a subset of the primary key.)

The relation in Fig. 9.4 is in the first normal form but not in the second.

Author is not functionally dependent on book number, but the other attributes are functionally dependent on book number. We can put this relation into the second normal form by forming a separate table for book numbers and authors, as shown below. This eliminates much of the redundancy.

81

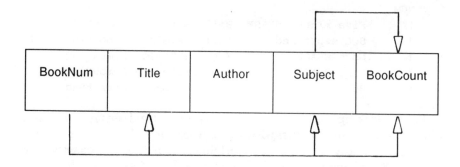

Fig 9.4 Relation in the first normal form only.

BOOKNUM	TITLE	SUBJECT	BOOKCOUNT
1	Five minute dBASE	Computing	3
2	SQL explained	Computing	3
3	More dBASE	Computing	3
3	More dBASE	Computing	3
4	How to sell	Marketing	1

BOOKNUM	AUTHOR
1	Bill Garth
2	Philip Klein
3	Mike la Salle
3	Hans Pietersen
4	John Scarman

However, this design still leaves a number of problems (or **anomalies**) to be resolved:

(a) Insertion anomaly. There is no way of adding a new subject category without at the same time adding a book to that category.

(b) Change anomaly. If the number of books in a category changes, we would have to alter several different rows.

(c) Deletion anomaly. When we delete the data for a book, we are losing the count of the books in the category.

These anomalies come about because the book count attribute is not only functionally dependent on book number, but also on subject category, which is in turn dependent on book number. This situation is described by the term **transitive dependence**.

Normalisation theory

A relation is in the third normal form if it is in the second normal form, and if it contains no transitive dependencies.[1]

In order to convert our library database to the third normal form, we would have to separate out a new relation containing the subject and book count attributes (Fig 9.5).

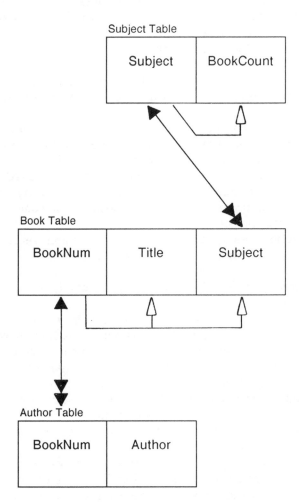

Fig. 9.5 Relation in the third normal form.

---

[1]Put another way, a relation is in the third normal form if there exists a primary key (which might consist of a combination of attributes) which identifies a specified entity and a number of attributes which that entity describes. The attributes which describe the entity must be dependent on the whole key and on nothing other than the key.

The definition of the third normal form does not take account of the fairly exceptional situation in which: a relation includes more than one **candidate** key (a candidate key is any attribute or combination of attributes which could serve as a primary key); the candidate keys are made up different attributes; and they have at least one attribute in common.[1] The Sales table is an example of this.

This problem leads to the next stage in the hierarchy of normal forms: the **Boyce–Codd** normal form. The definition of the Boyce–Codd normal form makes use of the concept of **determinants**. A determinant is an attribute, or combination of attributes, on which another attribute is completely functionally dependent. A relation is in the Boyce–Codd normal form when each determinant is a candidate key.

Fourth and fifth normal forms also exist. These have a much more theoretical significance than the first, second, third and Boyce–Codd normal forms, and are outside the scope of this book.

The theory of normalisation should not be allowed to take precedence over practical considerations. Eliminating transitive dependencies will promote an elegant design, but sometimes it is simply not worth the bother.

Good practice has to be governed by common sense. A good example of this is when several items of data are always used as whole. In this case, it is not usually sensible to spread them over several different tables, however elegant this looks in terms of normalisation theory.

Consider a relation containing these attributes: name, (street) address, town, postcode. The relation is not in the third normal form because transitive dependencies exist. In particular, the town is not only functionally dependent on the primary key (name-address-town) but also on the postcode. But the postcode is in turn functionally dependent on the primary key. (If we took name-address-postcode to be the primary key, the relation would not even be in the second normal form, since in this case the town would be dependent on one of the parts of the primary key.)

In order to achieve the third normal form, we would have to sub-divide the relation, as shown in Fig. 9.6. Given that the name, street address, town and postcode are always used on combination, sub-dividing the relation in this way does not really make sense.

It is tempting to think of the design process as one in which you start with the first normal form, then gradually refine it until you reach the third normal form. In practice, things are not done like

---

[1]Date (1990), p543.

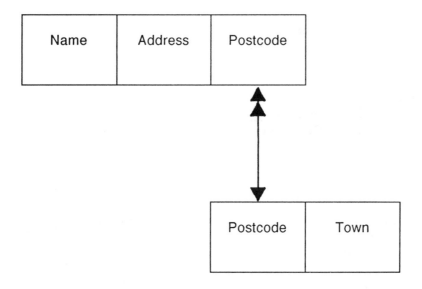

Fig 9.6 A not-very-sensible normalisation of an address relation.

this. An experienced designer will start with a semantic analysis of all the obvious entities, characteristics and relationships, and then proceed to a design in the third normal form more or less intuitively.

9.6 Entity-relationship diagrams

During the process of semantic analysis, some designers make frequent use of **entity-relationship diagrams**. In these diagrams, entities are represented by rectangles and relationships by diamonds. The depiction of relationships also includes their degree of association (whether it is one-to-many, many-to-many, etc.). The characteristics of entities are shown by ellipses.

There is no completely perfect criterion for deciding whether something is an entity (that is, an identifiable object) or a relationship. In the example shown in Fig. 9.7, a transaction is an entity, but it could also be considered a relationship. In an entity-relationship diagram, a relation can also have characteristics.

85

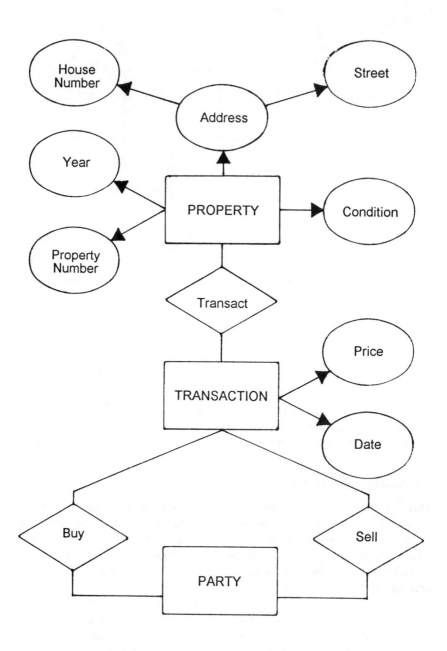

Fig. 9.7 Example of an entity-relationship diagram.

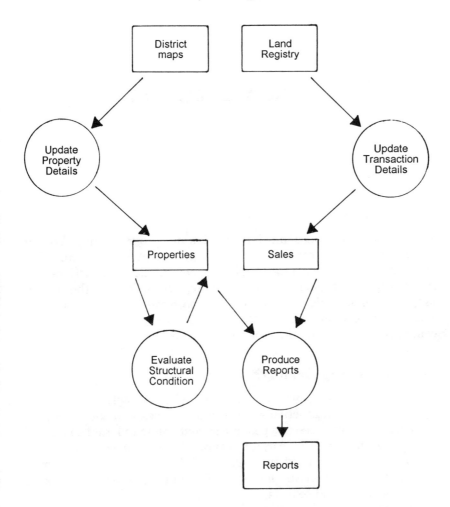

Fig 9.8 Example of a data-flow diagram.

9.7 Data-flow diagrams

A **data-flow diagram** (DFD) can be a useful tool during the initial analysis of information flows.[1] A DFD shows manual processes as well as automatic ones (see example in Fig. 9.8). There is no attempt to depict a time dimension in a DFD.

---

[1]DeMarco (1978).

CHAPTER TEN

Elementary programming

10.1 Introduction

This chapter provides an introduction to programming. We will discuss the basic principles of the topic, including program flow, decision making, looping, variables, expressions, functions and input/output. Throughout the chapter, we will use the dBASE language in its role as a general-purpose programming language, rather like Pascal, etc. In Chapter 11, we will look at ways of combining dBASE and SQL for use in database-oriented applications.

10.2 What is programming?

In earlier chapters, we saw how dBASE IV/SQL can be used interactively. In interactive work, the user types in a command, sees the results on the screen, types in the next command, and so on. This is usually the simplest way of obtaining quick answers to *ad hoc* queries. But if you need to carry out a particular procedure many times, this interactive method of working tends to become time-consuming and tedious.

In many routine activities, the user is obliged to type the same commands over and over again. What we really need is some way of typing these commands just once, saving them in a file, then, as it were, playing them back each time we need them. In its simplest form, this is exactly what programming is all about.

When you create a program, you type normal SQL or dBASE commands, but instead of typing them at a prompt, you enter them into a text file. When you run the program, each command in the file is executed in turn. A program, then, is essentially a sequence of instructions which have been stored in a file and which can be executed on demand.

In the following pages, we will see how to construct a program and

```
 Layout   Words   Go To   Print   Exit                    2:28:03 pm
[········▼1·▌····▼··2····▼····3··▼······4▼·······▼5·····▼··6····▼····7··▼·······
select Count(*), Max(Price), Min(Price), Avg(Price), Sum(Price)
from Sales;




Program  C:\dbase\data\SUMMARY   Line:2 Col:12              σ              Ins
```

Fig. 10.1 The text editor.

how to put it to work. In doing so, we will make use of dBASE IV's built-in text editor, which you invoke with the MODIFY FILE command (this can abbreviate this to MODI FILE).

The first step is to type, at the SQL or dot prompt: MODIFY FILE followed by the name of the program which you wish to create. After you have typed the name, press Enter.

The program name must follow these rules:

(a) It must not exceed eight characters.
(b) No spaces are allowed in the name.
(c) The extension .PRS must be added to the name. This tells dBASE IV that the file is a program, and that it contains SQL instructions.
(d) The name must not be the same as the name of the 'alternate' file, if such a file is in use (this is the file which is opened with the SET ALTERNATE command; see Section 3.6).

An example of a program name is SUMMARY.PRS. To create this file with dBASE IV's built-in editor, you would type the following:

```
MODIFY FILE SUMMARY.PRS
```

After entering this command, you will see an empty text-editing screen. To create the program, you type normal SQL commands into this screen, for example as shown in Fig. 10.1. (For detailed instructions for using the editor, refer to Appendix A.)

89

When you have finished typing the SQL commands, you press Ctrl-End to close the editor and save the file.

In order to see the program working, you issue a DO command. This consists of the word DO, followed by the name of the program (without the .PRS extension). For example:

```
DO SUMMARY
```

At this stage, dBASE IV checks the **syntax** of the program, that is, it checks that the SQL commands in the program conform to the normal rules of the language. If it finds an error in the syntax, it displays an explanatory message.

If there are no syntax errors, dBASE IV proceeds to **compile** the program. This involves converting it to a more compact form which it can execute faster.[1]

The compilation process will take a few moments, especially if it is a long program. However, this is a once-only task. The compiled version of the program is held in a file and can be used as often as you like. The file has the same name as the original program, but with the extension .DBO. In the example that we have been using, the compiled program would be called SUMMARY.DBO.

If you alter the original program, dBASE IV will re-compile it automatically. Whenever you use the built-in editor to alter an existing program file, dBASE IV checks to see if the corresponding .DBO file exists (in this example, it would check for the existence of SUMMARY.DBO if you altered SUMMARY.PRS). If the file does exist, dBASE IV will delete it. Then, the next time that you issue a DO command to run the program, dBASE IV will automatically create a new compiled version.

10.2.1 A useful little program

When using a database, it is often desirable to obtain basic information about the tables and columns which the database contains. This information is held in the database's catalogue tables. It can be accessed with the following SQL

```
SELECT colname, coltype, collen, tbname
FROM syscols WHERE NOT tbname LIKE 'SYS%';
```

---

[1]dBASE IV is a 'pseudo-compiler'. Either dBASE IV itself or a runtime module is required in order to run the compiled program (a runtime module is a special version of dBASE IV which can only run programs). By contrast, a 'true' compiler can produce programs in a language which the computer can execute directly.

It would be tedious to have to type this same command each time that you wanted to know a table or column name. The command is therefore a good candidate for making into a program. To do this, just issue a MODIFY FILE command to call up the editor, specifying a suitable name for the program (e.g. INFO.PRS). Then type in the command and save the file. From now on, whenever you need information from the catalogue tables, you only need to type:

```
DO INFO
```

Of course, in order to be able to use the program, the relevant database must already have been opened.[1]

10.3 SQL alone is not enough

SQL is primarily a language for working with databases: for creating them, keeping them up to date, and above all for performing searches on them. But if you want to develop a complete self-contained system (or **application**), then SQL on its own will not be adequate.

A complete application is likely to include a number of functions which cannot be programmed with SQL. An obvious example is a menu. Most applications need some way of showing the user a list of the available functions, and of asking the user to make a choice from this list. SQL has no facilities for doing this.

The following is an example of a menu, of the sort which might be displayed by an application which uses our sample Housing database.

```
Housing Information System

A = Alter the data
N = New properties
Q = Queries
S = Summaries
X = Exit the system

What is your choice:
```

---

[1]The program is associated with whatever database was open at the time that the program was compiled. It can therefore only work with that one database. If you wanted to use INFO.PRS with another database, you would have to delete the compiled version (you can do this with the command ERASE INFO.DBO). The next time that you issued the command DO INFO, the program would be re-compiled. It would then be associated with whatever database was open at that point, and would provide information about that database.

Another function which SQL does not support is the data-entry form. This is an on-screen form, designed to make it easy for users to enter data, such as details of new properties (see Fig. 10.2). The form might be invoked from the menu. As each field is filled in, the relevant values are stored in the table. When the user has finished entering data, the form is cleared and the menu returns.

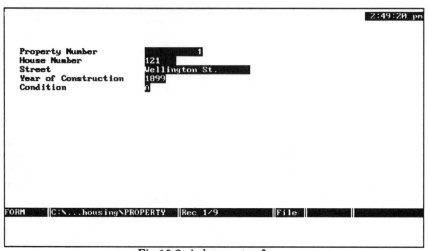

Fig 10.2 A data-entry form.

One further ability which SQL lacks is **looping**, that is, the ability to go back to an earlier function or process and to carry it out again. For example, the application might ask the user to make a choice from the menu, do whatever the user chose, then go back and ask for a choice again.

SQL then offers no facilities for communicating with the user, for dealing with user choices, and for performing tasks which involve looping. For these jobs, we need to seek help from a second language. Usually this is done by using a general-purpose programming language like Cobol or C. A common practice is to use these other languages for writing the main part of the application programs, but to incorporate SQL for the database handling functions. This is known as **embedded SQL**.

Many database management systems, however, incorporate their own programming language alongside SQL. This is the case with dBASE IV.

The dBASE programming language was created by Wayne Ratliff, an American programmer who, in his spare time, developed a database package called Vulcan. This package was eventually taken over by a software publisher, Ashton-Tate, who marketed it under

92

the name of dBASE II. This was to become the most popular database package on microcomputers. dBASE II later developed into dBASE III, dBASE III Plus and dBASE IV.

The dBASE language is a very comprehensive language. It has all the features of a general-purpose programming language, including decision-making and looping. It also has features which make it easy to communicate with users in a friendly way. Above all, it can be used as a query language in its own right, with the ability to create and maintain databases, and to retrieve, edit and delete records.

However, the query language features of dBASE are less powerful than those of SQL. In particular, dBASE requires that you specify in much more detail the exact way in which it must find a required item of data. SQL, on the other hand, generally takes care of the details for you.

In this book, we use SQL as much as possible, using the dBASE language to fill in the gaps where SQL falls short. Because it is not possible to use commands from the query language part of dBASE in .PRS programs, we will cover dBASE's own query language commands in passing only.

In the remainder of this chapter, we will use the dBASE language to examine some of the general principles of programming. We will also explore the possibilities which the language has for communicating with the user.

10.4 Displaying text on the screen

The time-honoured way of demonstrating the basic aspects of a programming language is to write a short program which does nothing more than display the words 'Hullo world' on the screen. So let's do just that.

With the help of the built-in text editor (invoked with MODIFY FILE), we create a text file, with the name GREETING.PRS. The file will contain the following two lines:

```
* Greeting.Prs. Display Hullo World on the screen
? 'Hullo world'
```

The question mark (in the second line) is a dBASE command. (For convenience, we will use the term 'dBASE command' to mean any command which belongs to the dBASE language rather than the SQL language.) The question mark means: go to the next line on the screen (the one after the line currently containing the cursor) and display whatever appears in the command after the question mark. If the item after the question mark is the actual text to be displayed (as in this example), it must be enclosed in quotation marks. dBASE has several other commands for displaying text on the screen, and we will look at some of them later.

The first line in our program (the one beginning with an asterisk) is a comment. A comment is not executed by the computer. Instead, it contains explanatory text for the benefit of people reading the program. Good comments help other programmers to understand what a program does and how it works. They also help programmers to understand their own programs when they look at them again in the future. The comment shown in this example represents the absolute minimum: the name of the program and a brief note of its function.

In order do see the results of this program on the screen, you issue the command:

```
DO GREETING
```

dBASE IV proceeds to compile the program, then executes it. The program displays the following text on the screen:

```
Hullo world
```

10.5 Obtaining input from the user

As well as displaying information **to** the user, the program can obtain information **from** the user. This is best demonstrated by the following somewhat trivial example.

In this example, the program displays a message to prompt the user to enter something:

```
Please type a word:
```

After this message has been displayed, the cursor will appear immediately to its right. The program now waits for the user's input. After the user has typed the word and pressed the Enter key, the program proceeds to the next step, which is to display the message:

```
You have typed:
```

followed by the word that the user entered.

So if the user entered the word 'rhubarb', the entire dialogue would appear as follows:

94

```
Please type a word: rhubarb
You have typed:
rhubarb
```

The program looks like this:

```
* Echo.Prs. Get text from the user and re-display it
ACCEPT 'Please type a word: ' TO word
? 'You have typed:'
? word
```

This program introduces a new command: ACCEPT. The ACCEPT command does three separate things:

(a)   It displays a small piece of text on the screen. In this case, it displays 'Please type a word:'.

(b)   It causes the program to pause until the user has typed something. The program continues only when the user presses the Enter key.

(c)   Finally, it stores the user's input in a **variable**. If this variable does not already exist, the command creates it.

10.5.1 Variables

A variable can best be described as a pigeon-hole in the computer's memory: a place where information can be stored on a temporary basis. You can only store information in this way by creating a variable to hold the information. In doing so, you must also specify a name for the variable.

In the dBASE language, variable names are subject to a maximum of 10 characters. The name may contain any combination of letters, digits and the underscore character, but it must begin with a letter. Spaces are not allowed within the variable name.

Here are some examples of valid variable names:

```
choice
quantity
quantity1
quant_1
```

and of some **invalid** variable names:

```
3Quant (must begin with a letter)
possibilities (more than ten characters)
quant 1 (may not contain a space)
```

95

Choose variable names carefully. A good choice of name is one which reminds you exactly what the variable is for. This also applies to names of tables, columns, etc. It is also important not to use the same name for different things, as this will cause confusion and can lead to errors.

Like the columns in a table, every variable has a distinct data type. In dBASE, a variable's data type is established at the point at which the variable is created. The available types are character, numeric, logical and date.

Let's look again at the ACCEPT command. Its general form is:

```
ACCEPT prompt TO variable
```

The command displays whatever text is specified as the prompt. It then waits for the user to type something. As soon as the user enters some text and presses the Enter key, the command places that text into the variable. The variable in the ACCEPT command is always a character type.

In our example program, we used the command:

```
ACCEPT 'Please type a word: ' TO word
```

In this case, the prompt consists of the message asking the user to type the word. (Note the extra space at the end of the message. This helps to separate the user's input from the prompt, thus improving readability.) The variable is called 'word' and is a character type.

The two commands which follow the ACCEPT command in the example program both display text on the screen:

```
? 'You have typed:'
```

This displays an actual piece of text, this being the message 'You have typed:', on a new line.

```
? word
```

This displays whatever is currently held in the variable called 'word'. dBASE knows that the item following the question mark is a variable because it does not appear within quotation marks. You would use quotation marks to indicate that the actual text in the program is the text which is to be displayed (as in the previous ? command).

96

Let's now look at a slightly more elaborate program.

```
* Admit.Prs. Help with making a confession
ACCEPT 'What is your last name: ' TO LastName
ACCEPT 'What is your first name: ' TO ForeName
?
? 'I, '
?? ForeName
?? ' '
?? LastName
? 'admit to having stolen a bicycle.'
```

This program will produce a dialogue such as the following:

```
What is your last name: Rushworth
What is your first name: Frank

I, Frank Rushworth
admit to having stolen a bicycle.
```

Now let's examine this program in detail.

```
ACCEPT 'What is your last name: ' TO LastName
ACCEPT 'What is your first name: ' TO ForeName
```

These commands display the relevant prompts and create two variables, LastName and ForeName, to hold the user's input.

```
?
```

A question mark on its own moves the cursor down one line, thus inserting a blank line in the output.

```
? 'I, '
```

This small piece of text will appear on the next line.

```
?? ForeName
```

When two question marks appear together like this, the text is displayed at the current cursor position rather than on a new line. This command therefore displays the contents of the ForeName variable immediately after the previous text.

97

```
?? ' '
```

This simply outputs a space, on the same screen line as the previous items.

```
?? LastName
```

Still on the same line, this displays the contents of the LastName variable.

```
? 'admit to having stolen a bicycle.'
```

This piece of text will appear on a fresh line.

10.6 Character-type expressions

An **expression** is a combination of values of a given data type. The expression itself has the same data type as the individual values (with one or two minor exceptions). An expression is therefore of type character (or text), numeric, logical or date.

Values in an expression are combined by means of **operators**.

In character expressions, the most important operator is the plus sign, which is used to join two pieces of text together.

In the following example, a ? command is used with an expression, to replace four separate ? commands.

```
* Admit2.Prs. Help with making a confession
* Alternative version
ACCEPT 'What is your last name: ' TO LastName
ACCEPT 'What is your first name: ' TO ForeName
?
? 'I, ' + ForeName + ' ' + LastName
? 'admit to having stolen a bicycle.'
```

This program is the same as the earlier example (ADMIT.PRS), except for the following line:

```
? 'I, ' + ForeName + ' ' + LastName
```

Here, an expression is formed from four elements: the text 'I, ', the contents of the ForeName variable, a single space, and the contents of the LastName variable. The result of the expression is displayed on the screen by means of the ? command.

10.7 The assignment operator

The assignment operator, which in dBASE is an equals sign, is used to store a value in a variable:

```
variable = value
```

If the variable does not already exist, the assignment process will create it.

An alternative form of assignment is a command of the form:

```
STORE value TO variable
```

The STORE command is preferable to the equals sign because the meaning of the command is much clearer (and, in programming, clarity is everything).

In the next example, we will store the result of a character expression in a variable.

```
* Admit3.Prs. Help with making a confession
* Another variation
ACCEPT 'What is your last name: ' TO LastName
ACCEPT 'What is your first name: ' TO ForeName
STORE 'I, ' + ForeName + ' ' + LastName TO Item_1
STORE 'admit to having stolen a bicycle.' TO Item_2
?
? Item_1
? Item_2
```

The fifth line of this program is an assignment:

```
STORE 'I, ' + ForeName + ' ' + LastName TO Item_1
```

This command contains an expression, formed from the four elements: 'I, ', the ForeName variable, the space between forename and last name, and the LastName variable. This is similar to the previous example, except that here the result of the expression is temporarily assigned to the variable named Item_1.

The next line is also an assignment:

```
STORE 'admit to having stolen a bicycle.' TO Item_2
```

Here, a simple piece of text is assigned to the variable Item_2.

99

The last two lines of the program display the contents of the variables, one beneath the other:

```
? Item_1
? Item_2
```

10.8 Forms

In order to help the user enter data into the program, the programmer can create a **form** on the screen.

A form contains a number of distinct boxes, each of which corresponds to one of the items to be entered (that is, to one **input field**). It can also include fixed text such as explanatory prompts and field labels.

When the user has finished filling in one field, the cursor goes on to the next one. The user can also move the cursor back to the fields which have already been completed, for example to correct earlier mistakes. The cursor control keys are used to move the cursor. The user can alter the existing contents of a field either by overtyping or inserting new characters.

When the user passes the cursor through the last field in the form (either by pressing Enter in the last field, or by filling the entire field with characters), the program transfers the data from the form to the relevant variables.

The programmer has full control over the design of the form. The location of each element of the form (text and input fields) is specified in the program by means of screen **co-ordinates**.

The first step in defining a form is to create a variable for each of the input fields. Recall that a variable can be created simply by storing a value in it. In the case of character variables, a suitable starting value is usually a string of spaces, the number of spaces in the string corresponding to the width of the field.

The location of the field (and of an accompanying prompt) is specified by means of a command like the following:

```
@ row, column SAY prompt GET variable
```

The row and column are numbers which indicate where on the screen the prompt is to appear. Rows are numbered from 0 (top row) to 24; columns are numbered from 0 (left-most column) to 79.[1]

---

[1]The @/SAY command can also be used simply to display information at a specified point on the screen. In this case, the GET clause would be omitted. See also 14.3.

Forms

After you have specified all the fields in this way, you issue the command:

```
READ
```

This command allows the user to fill in the form. When the command finishes (that is, when the user has finished the form), the variables will contain the text which the user entered.

The following example shows how this works in practice:

```
* Admit4.Prs. Help with making a confession
* Version using a form
STORE '                    ' TO ForeName
STORE '                    ' TO LastName
CLEAR
@ 5,3 SAY 'What is your last name:    ' GET ForeName
@ 6,3 SAY 'What is your first name:   ' GET LastName
READ
CLEAR
? 'I, '
? ForeName
? LastName
? 'admit to having stolen a bicycle.'
```

Let's look at this program in detail:

```
STORE '                    ' TO ForeName
STORE '                    ' TO LastName
```

These commands create the variables LastName and ForeName and fill them with spaces. Since we wish to use the variables to store text values, they must be of character type. This is achieved by assigning to each of them an initial value which is itself of character type, in this case, a string of spaces.

```
CLEAR
```

For clarity, the form should be displayed on an otherwise empty screen. The CLEAR commands clears the screen.

```
@ 5,3 SAY 'What is your last name:    ' GET ForeName
@ 6,3 SAY 'What is your first name:   ' GET LastName
```

These are the commands which actually create the form. The

101

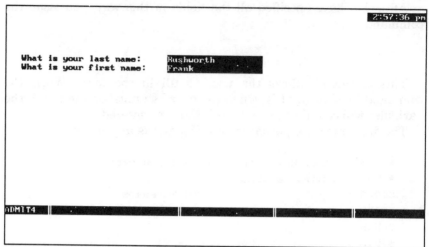

Fig. 10.3 A simple form.

prompts will appear at the specified locations, with the input fields to their immediate right. The items specified after the keyword GET are the variables which will hold the user's data.

READ

This command activates the form. Without the READ command, there is no way for the user to enter data into the form.

```
CLEAR
? 'I, '
? ForeName
? LastName
? 'admit to having stolen a bicycle.'
```

These commands display the results of the program, as in the earlier examples.

What actually happens when this program is run? First, the screen is cleared and the form is displayed. Next, control is passed to the user, who fills in the two fields (see Fig. 10.3). When the user presses Enter in the second field, the screen again clears (because of the second CLEAR command), and the following text is displayed:

```
I,
Frank
```

102

```
Rushworth
admit to having stolen a bicycle.
```

In this example, the ForeName and LastName variables are both character types. Their types were determined by the way in which they were initialised:

```
STORE '                         ' TO LastName
```

A numeric variable can be initialised in a similar way, for example:

```
STORE 0 TO Quantity
```

Because the value here is numeric, it must be written **without** quotation marks.

By default, a numeric variable in a form results in an input field which is 10 digits wide. However, you can override this by specifying a different length. You do this by adding a PICTURE clause to the end of the SAY/GET command:

```
@ 5,3 SAY "How many? ' GET Quantity PICTURE '######'
```

The number of hash marks in the string in the PICTURE clause tells dBASE the width of the input field in digits (six in this example). This in turn limits the number that can be input. If you want to allow the user to enter a number with a decimal point, place a full stop in the corresponding position in the PICTURE string. For example, to enter a number with up to three digits before the decimal point and two after it, the PICTURE clause would be:

```
PICTURE '###.##'
```

If you want to suppress the display of zero values in the field, place the characters @z before the string, separated from it by at least one space:

```
PICTURE '@Z ###.##'
```

This will still permit the user to enter a value of zero, but it will be displayed as a string of spaces.

If you want to allow the user to enter a date, you can initialise a date variable like this:

103

```
STORE {00/00/00} TO DueDate
```

And to initialise a logical variable:

```
STORE .F. TO YesOrNo
```

10.9 Numeric expressions

A numeric expression is a combination of numeric values. The result of a numeric expression is itself of numeric type.

The values in a numeric expression are combined by means of **mathematical operators**. For example:

```
4 + 5
```

is a numeric expression in which the plus sign is a mathematical operator. Table 10.1 lists all the mathematical operators.

Table 10.1. Mathematical operators

Operator	Meaning	Example	Value
+	addition	4.5 + 100.9	105.4
−	subtraction	99 − 77	22
*	multiplication	137 * 15	2055
/	division	4 / 2	2
^ or **	exponentiation	3 ** 2	9

In the expression:

```
4 + 5
```

the values 4 and 5 are called **constants**. As well as constants, a numeric expression can include numeric-type variables, as in the following examples:

```
STORE 4 TO Quant_1
STORE 5 TO Quant_2
STORE Quant_1 + Quant_2 TO Quant_3
```

Here two variables are created, Quant_1 and Quant_2, and values are assigned to them. The expression in the third line is then evaluated, and its result stored in another variable, Quant_3.

104

Numeric expressions

A numeric expression can include a mixture of mathematical operators. When this happens, multiplication and division are performed before addition and subtraction. So in the following example:

```
STORE 10 + 4 * 5 TO Quant
? Quant
```

the displayed value will be 30.

You can use parentheses to change the order in which the operations are performed. If part of the expression is enclosed in parentheses, that part is evaluated first, and its result is then used in the rest of expression:

```
STORE (10 + 4) * 5 TO Quant
? Quant
```

This time the result is 70.

The following program contains a numeric expression which includes numeric variables. The program asks the user to enter two numbers and displays their average.

```
* Average.Prs. Calculate an average.
STORE 0 TO Q1
STORE 0 TO Q2
CLEAR
@ 3,5 SAY 'Enter first value:  ' GET Q1
@ 4,5 SAY 'Enter second value: ' GET Q2
READ
? 'The average is: '
?? (Q1 + Q2) / 2
```

Let's look at the details:

```
STORE 0 TO Q1
STORE 0 TO Q2
```

The above command initialises the two numeric variables.

```
CLEAR
@ 3,5 SAY 'Enter first value:  ' GET Q1
@ 4,5 SAY 'Enter second value: ' GET Q2
READ
```

These commands display a form which asks the user for the two numbers.

```
? 'The average is: '
?? (Q1 + Q2) / 2
```

Finally, the average is calculated and displayed. Whenever an expression appears in a ? or ?? command, the expression is first evaluated and then the result is displayed.

A very common mistake is to try to combine a numeric data type with a character data type. It would be tempting to try to combine the last two lines in the above program in a single command:

```
? 'The average is: ' + (Q1 + Q2) / 2
```

This is **not** allowed and would lead to an error message.

However, constants and variables can be combined in the same expression if they are of the same data type. In the next example, a numeric constant value is added to the contents of a numeric variable:

```
STORE 10 TO Quantity
STORE Quantity + 5 TO Quantity
? Quantity
```

This would display 15.

10.10 Logical expressions

You can think of a logical expression as a statement that can be either true or false. It is analogous to the logical data type, which only ever has one of two values: true (which in the dBASE language is written as .T.) or false (written as .F.). A logical expression is an expression whose data type is logical.

Logical expressions are often based on comparisons. In this next example, the equals sign is used to compare two character variables:

```
STORE 'anything' TO Word1
STORE 'anything' TO Word2
? Word1 = Word2
```

The result would be .T. (true).

In the dBASE language, the equals sign is used in a somewhat unusual way when comparing character values. The comparison is considered to be true even if the string to the right of the equals sign is shorter than the string to the left, provided that the characters match within the length of the right-hand string. Thus:

```
? 'anything' = 'any'
```

would display .T. But, conversely:

```
? 'any' = 'anything'
```

would display .F.

You can change the way in which this comparison works by issuing the command:

```
SET EXACT ON
```

Once this command has been issued, the comparison is true only if the strings are equal both in value in length. Similarly

```
SET EXACT OFF
```

reverts to the other method.

The other relational operators can be used as well as the equals operator. You can also combine logical expressions with **logical operators** to form more complex expressions. In the dBASE language, these operators are .AND., .OR. and .NOT. They must always be written between full stops (this is not the case in SQL).

The following example contains an expression which is always true:

```
STORE .F. TO MustBe
? MustBe .OR. .NOT. MustBe
```

The result is .T.

```
STORE .T. TO MustBe
? MustBe .OR. .NOT. MustBe
```

The result is still .T.

By using brackets, you can alter the order in which the various parts of the expression are evaluated.

10.11 Functions

A **function** is a pre-defined operation which is carried out on an **argument**. The operation always returns a value.

The following is a small selection of the functions that are built into the dBASE language.

The UPPER function converts a piece of text to capitals. Its argument is the text to be converted. Its returned value is the same text in capitals:

```
STORE 'la bamba' TO SomeText
STORE UPPER(SomeText) TO SomeText
? SomeText
```

This prints LA BAMBA.

The opposite of UPPER is LOWER. The LOWER function converts its argument to lower-case letters.

The SPACE function returns a character string consisting of a string of spaces. The number of spaces is determined by the argument:

```
STORE SPACE(20) TO SpaceStr
```

This creates a variable called SpaceStr and fills it with twenty spaces.

The TRIM function removes any trailing spaces from a character string:

```
STORE 'Casa        ' TO LeftStr
STORE 'Blanca      ' TO RightStr
? TRIM(LeftStr) + SPACE(1) + RightStr
```

The result is:

```
Casa Blanca
```

The LTRIM function removes any leading spaces from a character string:

```
STORE 'Cat' TO LeftStr
STORE '         astrophe' TO RightStr
? LeftStr+LTRIM(RightStr)
```

108

The result is:

```
Catastrophe
```

The following example illustrates the use of some of these functions in a program:

```
* Admit5.Prs
* Variation to demonstrate functions
STORE SPACE(20) TO LastName
STORE SPACE(20) TO ForeName
CLEAR
@ 5,3 SAY 'What is your first name?  ' GET ForeName
@ 6,3 SAY 'What is your last name?   ' GET LastName
READ
STORE 'I, '+ TRIM(ForeName) + ' ' + ;¹
   TRIM(UPPER(LastName)) TO Item_1
STORE   'admit to having stolen a bicycle.' TO Item_2
?
? Item_1
? Item_2
```

Given the input:

```
Frank
Rushworth
```

the program would output this text:

```
I, Frank RUSHWORTH
admit to having stolen a bicycle.
```

Looking at the program in detail:

```
STORE SPACE(20) TO LastName
STORE SPACE(20) TO ForeName
```

The two variables, LastName and ForeName, are created and filled with spaces. This is done with the SPACE function.

---

[1]This line and the one immediately after it form a single command. When a semi-colon appears at the end of a line containing a dBASE command, the command is continued on the next line.

```
CLEAR
@ 5,3 SAY 'What is your first name?  ' GET ForeName
@ 6,3 SAY 'What is your last name?   ' GET LastName
READ
```

This creates the on-screen form, using the variable names specified in the two GET clauses.

```
STORE 'I, '+ TRIM(ForeName) + ' ' + ;
    TRIM(UPPER(LastName)) TO Item_1
```

In this line, an expression is used to assemble a text string. The ForeName and LastName variables initially contain 20 spaces each. If the names which the user enters are shorter than 20 spaces, the variables will be padded out with trailing spaces. These would cause an unsightly gap to appear in the middle of the name, so the TRIM function is used to remove them.

The expression also converts the last name to capitals. This is done with the UPPER function. This expression illustrates how functions can be **nested** (that is, when the result of one function becomes the argument of another).

10.11.1 dBASE functions in SQL commands

Several dBASE functions are useful when used within SQL commands.

The LEN function can be used to test the length of a character string. We can therefore use it to find out if a character variable or field is empty.

Query: In which rows of the Sales table has no Seller been entered?

```
SELECT *
FROM Sales
WHERE LEN(TRIM(Seller)) = 0;
```

The UPPER function can be used in queries to avoid discrepancies caused by the inconsistent use of capitals and lower case:

```
SELECT *
FROM Property
WHERE UPPER(Street) = 'WELLINGTON STREET';
```

However, this does not work in comparisons involving the keyword LIKE.

10.11.2 Type conversions

Having to deal with different data types can often lead to difficulties. For example, suppose that we wanted to write a program which calculates the average of two numbers, and for some reason we did not want to use a screen form. We would have to rely on the ACCEPT command to obtain the user's input. ACCEPT works with character-type variables. But averages are calculated by means of a numeric expression, and numeric expressions cannot contain character variables. Or maybe they can.

The solution is to use a type-conversion function. In this case, you would use the VAL function, which converts a variable from character to numeric.[1]

```
* Average1.Prs.
* Calculates an average. Demonstrates VAL function.
ACCEPT 'Enter first value:   ' TO Q1
STORE VAL(Q1) TO Q1
ACCEPT 'Enter second value: ' TO Q2
STORE VAL(Q2) TO Q2
? 'The average is: '
?? (Q1 + Q2) / 2
```

Conversely, it is possible to convert a numeric value to a character string. You do this with the STR function. An alternative way of writing the above program would be as follows:

```
* Average2.Prs.
* Calculates an average. Demonstrates STR function.
ACCEPT 'Enter first value:   ' TO Q1
STORE VAL(Q1) TO Q1
ACCEPT 'Enter second value: ' TO Q2
STORE VAL(Q2) TO Q2
? 'The average is: ' + STR((Q1 + Q2) / 2)
```

The STR function, as used in this example, will round the value to a whole number before converting it to a character string. By adding further arguments to the STR function, you can tell it to round the number to a given number of decimal places.

---

[1]If the user happened to type a letter in place of a digit, the program would fail because the argument of the VAL function must be a number. A more robust program would use a form to obtain the numbers from the user. A PICTURE clause could then be used to prevent the user from entering letters instead of digits.

In the next example, the number is rounded to two decimal places, then converted to a string of five characters (including the decimal point). Since the converted number only needs four character position, the string will include a leading space.

```
STORE 2.754 TO Quant
? STR(Quant,5,2)
```

The result is 2.75.

10.12 Decision making

In every example which we have looked at so far, the program simply executes the commands in sequence. It starts by executing the first instruction, then the next, and so on until it reaches the last instruction, at which point it stops. In practice, very few programs work this way. Most programs make decisions about which commands to execute according to the conditions which they encounter while they are running.

One way of providing the program with this decision-making ability is to use an IF/ENDIF construction:

```
IF condition
    commands
    .
    .
    .
ENDIF
commands
```

A condition (that is, a logical expression) must appear after the word IF. When the program reaches the line containing the IF, it evaluates the expression. If the expression is true, the program executes the commands which appear between the IF and the ENDIF. If it is false, the program jumps over these commands. After the ENDIF, these two paths come together again.

Here is an example:

```
* Polite.Prs. Demonstrates IF/ENDIF
CLEAR
? 'State whether you prefer'
? 'to be addressed politely'
ACCEPT 'Enter y or n: ' TO Choice
?
```

112

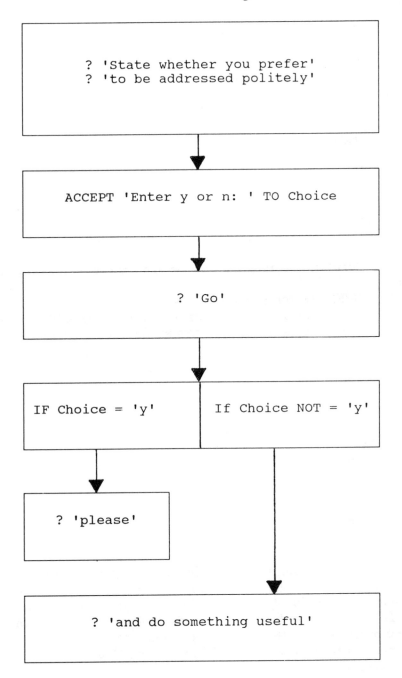

? 'State whether you prefer'
? 'to be addressed politely'

ACCEPT 'Enter y or n: ' TO Choice

? 'Go'

IF Choice = 'y'   If Choice NOT = 'y'

? 'please'

? 'and do something useful'

Fig. 10.4 Graphical representation of IF/ENDIF construction.

113

```
? 'Go'
IF Choice = 'y'
    ? 'please'
ENDIF
? 'and do something useful.'
```

An example of this program's dialogue:

```
State whether you prefer
to be addressed politely
Enter y or n: y

Go
please
and do something useful.
```

The 'logic' of the program can be represented graphically, as shown in Fig. 10.4.

The IF/ENDIF construction can be extended with the keyword ELSE. This allows us to specify one set of commands to be executed when the condition is true and another set for when it is false:

```
IF condition
    commands
    .
    .
    .
ELSE
    commands
    .
    .
    .
ENDIF
commands
```

When the program reaches the line containing the IF, it evaluates the condition, as before. If the condition is true, it executes the commands immediately following the IF, up to the line containing ELSE. It then skips the next commands, resuming execution with the first command after the ENDIF. If the condition is false, it skips the commands between IF and ELSE, executing those between ELSE and ENDIF.

The following example demonstrates this technique:

114

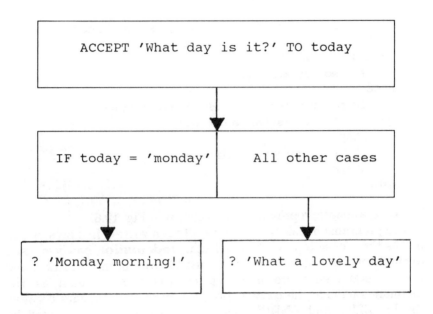

Fig. 10.5 Graphical representation of IF/ELSE/ENDIF construction.

```
* Days.Prs. Demonstrates IF/ELSE/ENDIF
ACCEPT 'What day is it?' TO today
IF today = 'monday'
    ? 'Monday morning!'
ELSE
    ? 'What a lovely day.'
ENDIF
```

Example output:

```
What day is it? tuesday
What a lovely day
```

Figure 10.5 shows the a graphical representation of this program.

It is also possible to nest these constructions, that is, to place one IF/ELSE/ENDIF inside another:

```
* Days2.Prs. Demonstrates nested IF/ELSE/ENDIF
ACCEPT 'What day is it? ' TO today
IF today = 'monday'
    ?  'Monday morning!'
ELSE
    IF today = 'sunday' .OR. today = 'saturday'
        ?  'It is the weekend.'
    ELSE
        ?  'Another working day.'
    ENDIF
ENDIF
```

The diagrammatic representation is shown in Fig. 10.6.

The programs in this section have all been written in a style which makes them easy to read. In particular, **indentation** has been used to emphasise their structure. The lines containing the IF, ELSE and ENDIF statements are lined up on the same column as the commands outside the construction; the lines that appears between the IF, ELSE and ENDIF statements have all been indented by several character positions. All this makes the logic of the program easier to grasp.

10.13 Decisions involving many choices

Sometimes, a program has to make a decision based on a large number of possible choices. A nested IF/ELSE/ENDIF construction can handle such cases, but if the nesting is more than a couple of levels deep, the whole thing can become unwieldy. In these circumstances, the DO CASE/ENDCASE construction provides a better solution:

```
DO CASE
    CASE condition 1
        commands
            .
            .
            .
```

116

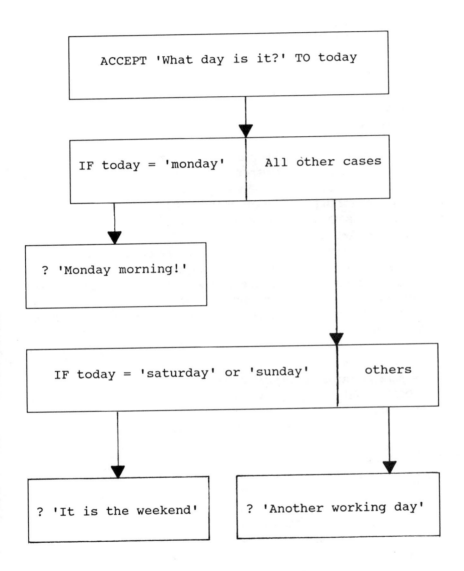

Fig. 10.6 Graphical representation of a nested IF/ELSE/ENDIF construction.

```
CASE condition 2
    commands
        .
        .
        .

CASE condition 3
    commands
        .
        .
        .

ENDCASE
commands
```

Here is how it works. When the program reaches the first CASE statement, it tests the corresponding condition. If it is true, the program executes all the commands up to the next CASE statement. It then jumps straight to the command following the ENDCASE. If the condition is false, the program repeats the procedure for the second CASE. And so on.

At most, the program will only recognise one of the conditions in a DO CASE/ENDCASE as true. Once the program has encountered a true condition and executed the corresponding commands, it will refrain from testing the other conditions. If none of the conditions is true, none of the commands within the construction will be executed.

Here is an example:

```
* Days3.Prs
* Demonstrates DO CASE/ENDCASE
ACCEPT 'Which day is it today? ' TO today
DO CASE
    CASE today = 'saturday' .OR. today = 'sunday'
        ? 'It is the weekend'
    CASE today = 'monday'
        ? 'Monday morning!'
    CASE today = 'tuedsay' .OR. today = 'wednesday'
        ? 'The week is still young'
    CASE today = 'thursday' .OR. today = 'friday'
        ? 'Soon be the weekend again'
ENDCASE
```

A variation of the DO CASE/ENDCASE construction is to add a line containing OTHERWISE. The commands between the OTHERWISE and the ENDCASE will be executed if none of the CASE conditions is true:

```
* Days4.Prs
* Demonstrates DO CASE/ENDCASE with OTHERWISE
ACCEPT 'Which day is it today? ' TO today
DO CASE
     CASE today = 'saturday' .OR. today = 'sunday'
          ? 'It is the weekend'
     CASE today = 'monday'
          ? 'Monday morning!'
     CASE today = 'tuedsay' .OR. today = 'wednesday'
          ? 'The week is still young'
     CASE today = 'thursday' .OR. today = 'friday'
          ? 'Soon be the weekend again'
     OTHERWISE
          ? 'I do not recongise what you have typed'
          ? 'Type the day in full, in lower case'
ENDCASE
```

10.14 Looping

Programs often need to execute the same sequence of commands many times. When the program reaches the end of the sequence, it **loops** back and executes the same commands again. This is repeated for as long as a specified condition is true.

In dBASE, this is achieved with the DO/ENDDO construction:

```
DO WHILE condition
     commands
     .
     .
     .
ENDDO
commands
```

When the program encounters the DO WHILE statement, it evaluates the condition. If it evaluates true, the program executes the commands on the lines immediately after the one containing the DO WHILE. When it reaches ENDDO, it loops back and repeats the process. When the condition eventually evaluates false, the program jumps to the command after the ENDDO.

The following program displays a greeting message twice, followed by a word of thanks:

```
* Loop.Prs
* Demonstrates a simple loop
```
119

```
* initialise the counter
STORE 0 TO Counter
* do for as long as the counter is less than 2
DO WHILE Counter < 2
    ? 'Good Morning'
    * increment the counter
    STORE Counter+1 TO Counter
ENDDO
? 'Thank you'
```

The program starts by creating a numeric variable, called Counter, and setting it to zero. It then reaches the line:

```
DO WHILE Counter < 2
```

The condition in this line is true because Counter is indeed less than two (it is zero). So the program continues with the next instruction, which is to display the greeting message. It then adds one to Counter.

When the program reaches the ENDDO statement, it loops back to the DO statement. The condition is still true (Counter is now one), so the next two instructions are performed a second time, that is, a second greeting is displayed and the counter is increased to two.

On reaching ENDDO the second time, the program again jumps back to the DO. This time the condition is false (Counter is now **equal to** two, not **less than** two). So the program jumps forward to the line after the ENDDO, at which point it prints the final Thank you.

In general terms, the variable which is tested in the DO condition (sometimes called a **control variable**) is first initialised in such a way that the condition is true when the program first evaluates it. As long as the condition remains true, the instructions 'inside the loop' will be executed. One of these instructions alters the control variable, in this case, by increasing it by one. At the end of the loop, the program branches back and tests the condition again. The whole thing is then repeated until the condition is no longer true.

In order to avoid an endless loop, something must eventually happen inside the loop which causes the condition to become false (at the point at which it is evaluated). The following is an example of an endless loop:

```
* Loop2.Prs
* An endless loop
```

```
STORE .T. TO Proceed
DO WHILE Proceed
    ? 'Hullo'
ENDDO
```

The logical variable Proceed in this example serves as the condition which determines whether or not the instructions between the DO and the ENDDO will be executed. In this case, it is initialised to .T. (true), so the instructions between the DO and the ENDDO will indeed be executed. However, nothing happens inside the loop to affect the value of Proceed. So the next time 'round the loop', the instructions will be executed again. And again, and again, forever (or until the computer is switched off).[1]

The lesson is that every loop must have an escape route. In this case, the escape route is implemented as follows:

```
* Loop3.Prs
* Loop which can be terminated
STORE .T. TO Proceed
DO WHILE Proceed
    ? 'Hullo'
    ACCEPT 'Do you want to finish now? ' TO Reply
    IF LOWER(Reply) = 'y'
        STORE .F. TO Proceed
    ENDIF
ENDDO
```

When the user answers 'y', the Proceed variable becomes .F. and the condition in the DO WHILE statement evaluates false. This causes the program to skip the instructions inside the loop, thus terminating the program.

The following program is a game which illustrates the use of a loop. The program picks a number at random, which the player must guess. At each incorrect guess, the program gives a clue to help the player. The example includes a number of functions which are described later.

```
* Game.Prs
* Number-guessing game; illustrates looping
SET TALK OFF
STORE RAND() TO Number
```

---

[1] A dBASE program can, however, be interrupted by pressing the Esc key. If you want to prevent users from doing this, issue the command SET ESCAPE OFF.

```
* This produces a random number between zero and one
STORE ROUND(Number,2) TO Number
* Round the number to two decimal places
STORE Number * 100 TO Number
* The number is now between zero and 100
? 'Guess a number between zero and 100'
STORE 0 TO Score
STORE .T. TO More
DO WHILE More
    ACCEPT 'What is your guess? ' TO GuesStr
    * With ACCEPT, only character data can be entered
    STORE Score + 1 TO Score
    STORE VAL(GuesStr) TO Guess
    * Type conversion is required for the comparison
     DO CASE
         CASE Guess > Number
            ? 'You are too high'
         CASE Guess < Number
             ? 'You are too low'
         CASE Guess = Number
             ? 'You are right'
             STORE .F. TO More
     ENDCASE
ENDDO
? 'Your score is: '
?? Score
```

Here is an example of the dialogue produced by this program:

```
Guess a number between zero and 100
What is your guess? 50
You are too high
What is your guess? 25
You are too low
What is your guess? 40
You are too low
What is your guess? 45
You are too low
What is your guess? 47
You are right
Your score is:        5
```

The program introduces two new functions. The RAND function, which has no argument, generates a random number between zero and one. It is useful in games and simulation programs. The ROUND functions rounds its first argument to the number of decimal places specified by its second argument.

10.15 Pseudocode, flowcharts and PSDs

When designing a complex program, it often helps to start by writing an outline to show the overall logic, postponing any consideration of the details until later. One way of writing an outline is to use **pseudocode**. This is an informal language which is half-way between a programming language and ordinary English. The following is a pseudocode outline of the guessing program:

```
Generate a random number between 0 and 100
Do the following until the number has been guessed
    Ask for a guess
    Increase the score by one
    If guess > number
        Tell them it is too high
    If guess < number
        Tell them it is too low
    If the guess = number
        Tell them it is right
        Make the loop terminate
End of Do loop
Tell them the score
```

Another way of planning the structure of a program is to draw a flowchart. Figure 10.7 shows an example.

A third possibility is to create a program structure diagram, or PSD, also called a Nassi–Schneidermann diagram. See Fig. 10.8 for an example.

10.16 Debugging

Debugging is the process of finding and correcting errors in programs. Most beginners are tempted to run their programs as soon as they have typed in the final line, with little or no thought as to how they will approach the testing. They often rely on good luck and hasty alterations to get the thing working. However, they soon realise that the only way to rid the program of errors is to approach the debugging process in an intelligent and systematic manner.

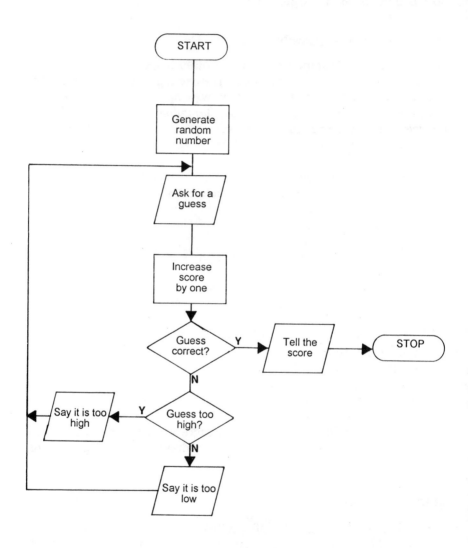

Fig. 10.7 Example of a flowchart.

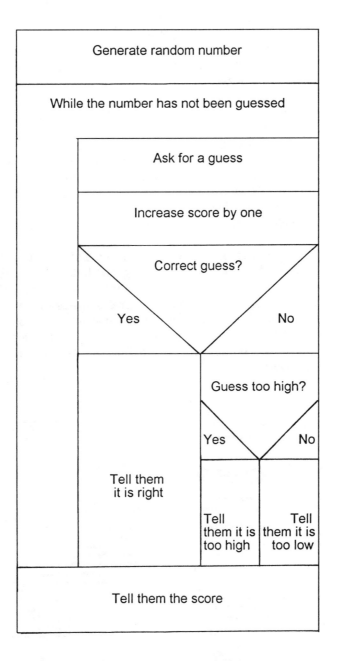

Fig. 10.8 Example of a PSD.

It is important to distinguish between several different kinds of errors. When you first test a newly typed program, you are most likely to be confronted with **syntax errors**. These are typically typing errors which appear as violations of the rules under which dBASE and SQL commands are constructed (e.g. a missing semi-colon). dBASE IV checks for syntax errors during the compilation process. When it detects an error, it displays an informative message which will help you to locate and correct the mistake. (These error messages can be recorded in an ALTERNATE file; see Section 3.6.)

When you have eliminated all the syntax errors, dBASE IV can finish compiling the program. It then runs the program. While the program is executing, you might encounter another type of error: a **runtime error**. These are errors which dBASE IV can only detect during program execution (e.g. a mismatched data type). When it encounters such an error, it halts the program, again displaying an informative message.

The third type of error is a **logical error**. This is an error which does not cause dBASE IV to halt the program, but which might result in the program not doing what it was intended to do. This could happen, for example, if an arithmetic expression was incorrect.

One way of tracking down runtime and logical errors is to execute the program one line at a time, pausing after each command to see exactly what it has done. You can do this by invoking dBASE IV's built-in **debugger**.

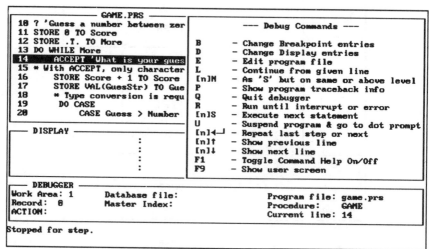

Fig. 10.9 The debugger screen.

Debugging

To start the debugger, type the command DEBUG followed by the name of the program, for example:

```
DEBUG Game
```

This will cause the debugger screen to appear, as shown in Fig. 10.9. The debugger displays the program at the top of the screen, with a highlight on the current line (initially the first line). By pressing S, you tell the debugger to execute this line and then to pause. Alternatively, you can press R to run the program until either a runtime error is detected or the Esc key is pressed. Other features of the debugger are briefly described in the help window in the top-right corner of the screen.

CHAPTER ELEVEN

Embedded SQL

11.1 Introduction

Every SQL command which can be executed interactively (that is, from the SQL prompt) can also be used within a dBASE program (a .PRS file). SQL also has several features which are intended to be used exclusively within programs.

Whenever SQL is used in combination with another programming language (in this case, the dBASE language), it is referred to as **embedded SQL**.

11.2 Passing values from dBASE to SQL

Embedded SQL allows variables to be used in commands in place of actual values. Specifically, at any point at which a constant value may be used, a variable name may be used instead. Consider, for example, the following command:

```
SELECT * FROM Property
WHERE Street = 'Wellington St.';
```

This could alternatively be written as:

```
STORE 'Wellington St.' TO StreetName
SELECT * FROM Property
WHERE Street = StreetName;
```

Here, the street name is first stored in a variable named StreetName. This variable is then used in the SELECT command, in place of the actual name.

We can take advantage of this technique to create a simple input program. Instead of forcing the user to type an SQL INSERT

128

command, the program would accept data into a form, then pass the data to SQL by means of variables.

Here is how it works. The program starts by creating new, empty variables for each of the columns in the table. We will call these variables VPropNum, VHouse, VStreet, VYear and VConditn respectively. The program then sets up a form for these variables, using the familiar @/SAY/GET and READ commands. The user uses the form to enter data into the variables. Finally, the program adds a new row to the table by means of the SQL INSERT command. Instead of using explicit values as it would in interactive SQL, the command works with the variables which the user has filled in.

```
* Input.Prs. Add a new row to the property table
CLEAR
STORE 0 TO VPropNum
STORE SPACE(6) TO VHouse
STORE SPACE(20) TO VStreet
STORE 0 TO VYear
STORE ' ' TO VConditn
CLEAR
@ 4,3 SAY 'Property Number          ' GET VPropNum
@ 5,3 SAY 'House Number             ' GET VHouse
@ 6,3 SAY 'Street                   ' GET VStreet
@ 7,3 SAY 'Year of Construction     ' GET VYear ;
   PICTURE '####'
@8,3 SAY 'Condition                ' GET VConditn
READ
INSERT INTO Property
VALUES(VPropNum,VHouse,VStreet,VYear,VConditn);
```

Note that, in the @/SAY/GET command for the year, there is a PICTURE clause:

```
@ 7,3 SAY 'Year of Construction' GET VYear ;
   PICTURE '####'
```

When an @/SAY/GET command is used with a numeric variable, dBASE IV normally displays a very wide box on the screen to hold the input field. The width of this box is determined by the maximum number of digits which dBASE uses to display numeric data. The PICTURE clause permits a specific field width to be stipulated, in this case four characters.

11.2.1 A query program

Having created an input program, it turns out that a query program is a simple variation on the same theme. In this example, the program invites the user to type in a house number and street name. These two items are stored in variables which are in turn used as the search targets in a SELECT command.

```
* Query.prs
* Asks the user for a house number and street name,
* then searches for this combination of values
CLEAR
STORE SPACE(6) TO VHouse
STORE SPACE(20) TO VStreet
@ 5,3 SAY 'House Number     ' GET VHouse
@ 6,3 SAY 'Street           ' GET VStreet
READ
CLEAR
SELECT * FROM Property
WHERE HouseNum =  VHouse
AND Street = VStreet;
```

The VStreet variable in this example is initialised to 20 spaces. This is because the street column in the Property table is 20 characters wide. The variable has to be big enough to allow the user to search for a name that occupies the full width of the column. On the other hand, it would be dangerous to make the variable wider than the column. When making comparisons, SQL takes account of any trailing spaces. If the variable had been set to 25 spaces, and if the user wanted to search for Wellington St., the variable would contain Wellington St. plus 11 spaces. But the table would contain Wellington St. plus six spaces. SQL would not consider these two values to be equal and the search would fail.

11.2.2 A more sophisticated query program

A difficulty with the query program shown above is that the user is always obliged to type in the street name in full. Apart from being time-consuming, this increases the likelihood of a typing error. We can overcome this by taking advantage of SQL's pattern-searching feature.

The following command would successfully locate rows containing, say, Wellington St., even if the complete name was not specified:

```
SELECT *
```

```
FROM Property
WHERE Street LIKE 'Welling*';
```

We can conduct the same type of search from inside a program by appending an asterisk to whatever the user types in.

However, there is a minor complication. The user is typing a value into a field which is 20 spaces wide. Because the value is unlikely to fill the field, surplus spaces will remain. Thus the program would search, for example, for:

```
'Welling               *'
```

which is not what we intended. The solution is to use the TRIM function to remove the trailing spaces before appending the asterisk.

Another improvement would be to arrange for the program to tell us if it was unable to find anything. It is a good rule for a program always to report its result in some way. This reassures the user.

Whenever SQL performs a SELECT, it stores a count of the number of rows which it finds. This figure is placed in a **system variable** and is available for use within the program. A system variable is similar to an ordinary variable, except that it is created automatically by dBASE IV/SQL.

The system variable which holds the count of the number of rows found is called SQLCNT. By testing this variable, the program can find out whether or not the SELECT was successful.

```
* Query1.Prs (more sophisticated version)
* Asks the user for a house number and street name,
* then searches for this combination of values
CLEAR
STORE SPACE(6) TO VHouse
STORE SPACE(20) TO VStreet
@ 5,3 SAY 'House Number  ' GET VHouse
@ 6,3 SAY 'Street        ' GET VStreet
READ
* In order to avoid having to enter the entire street
* name, an asterisk is appended to the entered value.
* Any trailing spaces must first be removed. This
* enables a pattern search to be performed, using LIKE.
STORE TRIM(VStreet) + '*' TO VStreet
CLEAR
SELECT * FROM Property
WHERE HouseNum = VHouse
```
131

```
AND Street LIKE VStreet;
IF SQLCNT = 0
    ? 'Cannot find anything'
ENDIF
```

11.3 Values passed from SQL to dBASE variables

In the previous section, we saw how values held in dBASE variables can be passed to SQL commands. By the same token, the values which SQL retrieves from a table can be passed back to dBASE variables. This is achieved by adding the INTO clause to the SELECT command. The clause specifies the names of the variables which are to receive the retrieved values.

In the following program fragment, the house number and street name from property number 1 are stored in two variables, named VHouse and VStreet respectively:

```
SELECT HouseNum, Street
INTO VHouse, VStreet
FROM Property
WHERE PropNum = 1;
```

If the variables named in the INTO clause do not already exist, the command will create them. If the SELECT command fails to find a row, the variables will not be created.

Bear in mind that a given variable can only hold one value at a time. If the SELECT returned more than one row, dBASE would not know which values to store in the variables.

SELECT/INTO can also be used to help alter the data in a table. In summary, the steps required to do this are as follows:

(a)   Select the row which is to be amended.
(b)   Store the values from the field in this row in variables.
(c)   Use the variables to create a form.
(d)   Let the user amend the contents of the variables via the form.
(e)   Store the data which is now on the screen back in the variables. The variables now contain the amended values.
(f)   Select again the row which is to amended.
(g)   Copy the contents of the variables to the corresponding fields in the selected row.

This strategy is used in the following program:

132

Values passed from SQL to dBASE variables

```
* Update.Prs. Asks for a property number; retrieves
* corresponding property; places house no., street,
* year, condition in variables by means of SELECT/INTO;
* displays the variables as part of a form, allowing
* their contents to be amended; returns updated values
* to the selected row. Will not work if there is more
* than one property with the same property number.
CLEAR
STORE 0 TO VPropNum
@ 4,3 SAY 'Property Number          ' GET VPropNum
READ
SELECT HouseNum, Street,YearC, Conditn
INTO VHouse, VStreet, VYear, VConditn
FROM Property
WHERE PropNum = VPropNum;
CLEAR
@ 5,3 SAY 'House Number          ' GET VHouse
@ 6,3 SAY 'Street                ' GET VStreet
@ 7,3 SAY 'Year of Construction  ' GET VYear ;
   PICTURE '####'
@ 8,3 SAY 'Condition             ' GET VConditn
READ
UPDATE Property
SET HouseNum = VHouse, Street = VStreet,
YearC = VYear, Conditn = VConditn
WHERE PropNum = VPropNum;
```

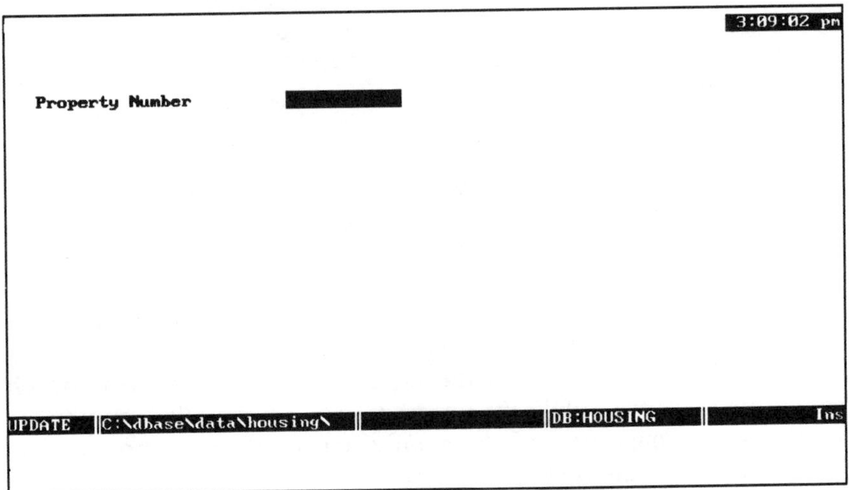

Fig. 11.1 First screen from the update program.

133

Embedded SQL

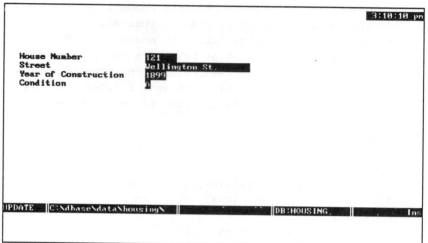

Fig. 11.2 Second screen from the update program.

When the program is run, the screen will initially appear as in Fig. 11.1. As soon as the user enters a value for the property number, the program displays a form showing the other values from the property's record (Fig. 11.2). This form can then be used to alter the data.

This update program works well enough, but it is not as robust as it might be. As we will see, it will fail under certain circumstances.

Suppose that the user typed in a property number which was not present in the table. The SELECT/INTO command:

```
SELECT HouseNum, Street,YearC, Conditn
INTO VHouse, VStreet, VYear, VConditn
FROM Property
WHERE PropNum = VPropNum;
```

would not find a row. Normally this command creates the variables VHouse, VStreet, VYear and VConditn. But if the command does not succeed in finding a row, then no such variables will be created. However, the rest of the program assumes that the variables now exist. The program will therefore eventually halt, complaining that it cannot find one or other of the variables that it requires.

This is an example of a runtime error, that is, an error which cannot be identified while the program is being compiled, only while it is running. Some runtime errors only emerge after the program has been in use for some time.

A second problem can occur if the command finds more than one

134

row. The program would only display the first row that meets the search condition but it would update all the rows which meet the condition in the UPDATE command.

The following program shows how to deal with these two problems. First, let us look at the structure of the program in pseudocode.

```
Perform a normal SELECT
Test the number of rows which it returned
If no rows returned
    Advise the user that the property could not be
    found
    Do not go any further
If more than one row returned
    Advise the user that the update cannot be done
    Do not go any further
If exactly one row returned
    Proceed with the update
```

This is what the program itself looks like:

```
* Update2.Prs
* Improved version
CLEAR
STORE 0 TO VPropNum
@ 4,3 SAY 'Property Number          ' GET VPropNum
READ
SELECT *
FROM Property
WHERE PropNum = VPropNum;
DO CASE
    CASE SQLCNT = 0
        ? 'There is no such property number.'
        WAIT 'Press any key to proceed.'
    CASE  SQLCNT > 1
        ? 'More than one property with this number.'
        ? 'The update is not possible.'
        WAIT 'Press any key to proceed.'
    CASE SQLCNT = 1
        SELECT HouseNum, Street,YearC, Conditn
        INTO VHouse, VStreet, VYear, VConditn
        FROM Property
        WHERE PropNum = VPropNum;
        CLEAR
        @ 5,3 SAY 'House Number          ' GET VHouse
```

135

```
@ 6,3 SAY 'Street                         ' GET VStreet
@ 7,3 SAY 'Year of Construction          ' GET VYear ;
  PICTURE '####'
@8,3 SAY 'Condition                      ' ;
  GET VConditn
READ
UPDATE Property
SET HouseNum = VHouse, Street = VStreet,
YearC = VYear, Conditn = VConditn
WHERE PropNum = VPropNum;
    ENDCASE
```

11.3.1 The WAIT command

You might have noticed the following line occurring twice in the above program:

```
WAIT 'Press any key to proceed.'
```

One of the most annoying things that a programmer can do to a user is to flash the output of the program on to the screen and then to clear the screen before the user can read it. The WAIT command gives the user the opportunity to read the screen at leisure.

WAIT is similar to ACCEPT in that both commands display a prompt and both create character-type variables. In the case of WAIT, the variable is optional (it is not used in this example). The WAIT command, however, accepts a single keystroke; the program resumes as soon as that key is pressed. With ACCEPT, an entire string may be entered and the program resumes only after the Enter key has been pressed.

11.4 Cursors

The SELECT command in SQL is oriented towards retrieving groups or **sets** of records. The dBASE language, on the other hand, can only work with a single record at a time. We have already seen one implication of this: the fact that the SELECT/INTO construction only works if you can be sure that it will retrieve exactly one row.

In order to build a bridge between SQL's set-oriented approach and the one-record-at-a-time way in which other languages work, SQL offers a feature called the **cursor**.

A cursor resembles the result table which is produced by the SELECT command. The difference is that the cursor can be accessed on a row-by-row basis.

The first thing that you must do with a cursor is to declare it. You do this with a command whose general form is as follows:

```
DECLARE cursor name CURSOR
FOR select command;
```

The command specifies a name for the cursor. It also specifies the rows and columns which the cursor is to contain. These are defined by the SELECT command which is embedded within the DECLARE command. The rows and columns of the cursor are the same as the rows and columns of this SELECT command's result table.

Before you can use the cursor, you must open it. This is achieved with a command in the following form:

```
OPEN CURSOR cursor name;
```

When the cursor is opened, the SELECT command is executed.[1]

Once the cursor has been opened, its rows can be accessed by means of a FETCH command, the general form of which is as follows:

```
FETCH cursor name
INTO variable(s);
```

The FETCH command always retrieves one row from the cursor. The values from this row are stored in the specified variables.

You can think of a cursor as a result table with a pointer attached. Before the FETCH command is executed for the first time, the pointer does not point to any particular row. After the first FETCH command, it moves to the first row of the result table. It is the data from this row which will be transferred to the variables. Each subsequent time that the FETCH is executed, the pointer advances one row. In each case, the data from the pointed-to row is stored in the variables. This continues until the data from the last row has been transferred. Note that there is no way for a cursor to move backwards.

In order to access successive cursor rows, the FETCH command would normally be issued from inside a loop. Clearly, there must be some way of finding out when the last row of the cursor has been processed, otherwise the program would get trapped in an endless

---

[1]The SELECT command is not executed when the cursor is declared. The rows in the cursor are those which exist when the OPEN CURSOR command is issued, not when the DECLARE command is executed.

loop. You can find out when you reach the last row by testing a system variable called SQLCODE, which reports the outcome of an embedded SQL command.

SQLCODE can take one of three values:

(a)   If the FETCH was successful, that is, if it succeeded in transferring values from the cursor to the variables, SQL sets SQLCODE to zero.

(b)   If the FETCH failed because there were no more rows in the cursor, SQL sets SQLCODE to 100.

(c)   If the FETCH failed because an error was detected, SQL sets SQLCODE to minus one.

This means that you can terminate the loop as soon as SQLCODE has a non-zero value.

After the cursor has been used, it should be closed with a command in the form:

```
CLOSE cursor name;
```

If the cursor is subsequently re-opened, the pointer will once again be at the first row.

The next program demonstrates the use of a cursor. This program simply lists the names of all streets, one below another, separated by an asterisk.

```
* Streets.Prs
* Produces a list of streets separated by asterisks
CLEAR
STORE SPACE(20) TO VStreet
DECLARE MyCursor CURSOR
FOR SELECT Street
FROM Property;
OPEN MyCursor;
STORE .T. TO Ok
DO WHILE ok
    FETCH MyCursor INTO VStreet;
    IF SQLCODE = 0
        ? VStreet
        ? '*'
    ELSE
        STORE .F. TO Ok
    ENDIF
ENDDO
```

```
CLOSE MyCursor;
```

Let us examine this program in detail:

```
STORE SPACE(20) TO VStreet
```

This creates an empty variable.

```
DECLARE MyCursor CURSOR
FOR SELECT Street
FROM Property;
```

A cursor named MyCursor is declared, containing the street name from each row in the Property table.

```
OPEN MyCursor;
```

Here the cursor is opened.

```
STORE .T. TO Ok
DO WHILE ok
    FETCH MyCursor INTO VStreet;
    IF SQLCODE = 0
        ? VStreet
        ? '*'
    ELSE
        STORE .F. TO Ok
    ENDIF
ENDDO
```

This is the main loop of the program. It accesses each row in the cursor in turn for as long as the Ok variable is true. The cursor has just one column: Street. Each time round the loop, the value of the Street column is placed in the VStreet variable. If the FETCH succeeds, the contents of VStreet are displayed on the screen, followed by an asterisk. When the FETCH fails, the program sets the Ok variable to false, so forcing the loop to terminate.

```
CLOSE MyCursor;
```

Finally, the program closes the cursor.

It is possible to specify a selection condition within the SELECT part of the DECLARE command. The following command declares a

139

cursor which will contain the house number, street, year and condition for all properties in Wellington Street:

```
STORE 'Wellington St.' TO WhichStr
DECLARE PropCur CURSOR
FOR SELECT HouseNum, Street, YearC, Conditn
FROM Property
WHERE Street = WhichStr;
```

11.4.1 Changing the rows in a cursor

We have seen how the information from a cursor can be stored in dBASE variables by means of the FETCH/INTO command. The reverse is also possible: new values can be inserted into the rows of the cursor.

To do this, you must first add the following clause to the DECLARE/CURSOR command:

```
FOR UPDATE OF column names
```

The column names in this clause are the ones whose values are to be updated. The clause comes at the end of the DECLARE command. An example:

```
DECLARE PropCur CURSOR
FOR SELECT HouseNum, Street, YearC, Conditn
FROM Property
WHERE Street LIKE WhichStr
FOR UPDATE OF HouseNum, Street, YearC, Conditn;
```

To actually update a row in the cursor with the new values, you use a variant of the UPDATE command. By adding the following clause to the UPDATE command, you stipulate that the row retrieved by the most recent FETCH is to be updated:

```
WHERE CURRENT OF cursor name
```

Here is an example of a complete UPDATE command:

```
UPDATE Property
SET HouseNum = NewNum, Street = NewStreet,
YearC = NewYear, Conditn = NewConditn
WHERE CURRENT OF PropCur;
```

This technique is applied in the next program. This is the same

140

update program, enhanced to allow the user to change several rows in turn. If the user entered a house number and street name of a property which had accidently been stored twice in the table, the program would not fail. The program presents the specified rows one by one in a form.

```
* Update3.Prs
* Prompts for a house number and street, then presents
* the corresponding rows in a form which the user can
* update
CLEAR
STORE SPACE(6) TO VHouse
STORE SPACE(20) TO VStreet
@ 5,3 SAY 'House Number          ' GET VHouse
@ 6,3 SAY 'Street                ' GET VStreet
READ
STORE TRIM(VStreet) + '*' TO VStreet
CLEAR
* Create a cursor for the row to be altered
DECLARE MyCursor CURSOR
FOR SELECT  HouseNum, Street, YearC, Conditn
FROM Property
WHERE  Street LIKE VStreet
AND HouseNum = VHouse
FOR UPDATE OF HouseNum, Street, YearC, Conditn;
OPEN MyCursor;
IF SQLCNT = 0
    WAIT 'Not found. Press any key to proceed.'
    STORE .F. TO Ok
ELSE
    STORE .T. TO Ok
ENDIF
* The following will be executed for each row in the
* cursor
DO WHILE Ok
    * Copies values from the rows to variables
    FETCH MyCursor
    INTO VHouse, VStreet, VYear, VConditn;
    IF SQLCODE <> 0
        STORE .F. TO Ok
    ELSE
        CLEAR
        * Use the variables to create a form for
```
141

```
* updating
@ 5,3 SAY 'House Number           ' GET VHouse
@ 6,3 SAY 'Street                  ' GET VStreet
@ 7,3 SAY 'Year of Construction   ' GET VYear ;
   PICTURE '####'
@ 8,3 SAY 'Condition               ' ;
   GET VConditn
READ
* Write the updated values back to the rows
UPDATE Property
SET HouseNum = VHouse, Street = VStreet,
YearC = VYear, Conditn = VConditn
WHERE CURRENT OF MyCursor;
   ENDIF
ENDDO
CLOSE MyCursor;
```

Let us look at the program line by line:

```
CLEAR
STORE SPACE(6) TO VHouse
STORE SPACE(20) TO VStreet
@ 5,3 SAY 'House Number           ' GET VHouse
@ 6,3 SAY 'Street                  ' GET VStreet
READ
STORE TRIM(VStreet) + '*' TO VStreet
CLEAR
```

This part of the program obtains the target address from the user.

```
DECLARE MyCursor CURSOR
FOR SELECT  HouseNum, Street, YearC, Conditn
FROM Property
WHERE   Street LIKE VStreet
AND HouseNum = VHouse
FOR UPDATE OF HouseNum, Street, YearC, Conditn;
```

This command creates the cursor which contains the house number, street, year and condition from the row to be altered.

```
OPEN MyCursor;
IF SQLCNT = 0
   WAIT 'Not found. Press any key to proceed.'
```

```
      STORE .F. TO Ok
ELSE
      STORE .T. TO Ok
ENDIF
```

Here the cursor is opened. If the cursor has no rows, SQLCNT will be set to zero. This can be used to warn the user that the required row was not found. In this case, the Ok variable is initialised to false. We can therefore ensure that the main loop (containing the FETCH command) is not executed when no row is found.

```
DO WHILE Ok
    * Copies values from the rows to variables
    FETCH MyCursor
       INTO VHouse, VStreet, VYear VConditn;
```

The values from the row are copied to variables.

```
    IF SQLCODE <> 0
        STORE .F. TO Ok
```

When the FETCH fails, SQLCODE will no longer be zero. This fact enables the program to know when the loop is to be terminated.

```
    ELSE
        CLEAR
        * Use the variables to create a form for
        * updating
        @ 5,3 SAY 'House Number          ' GET VHouse
        @ 6,3 SAY 'Street                ' GET VStreet
        @ 7,3 SAY 'Year of Construction  ' GET VYear ;
          PICTURE '####'
        @ 8,3 SAY 'Condition             ' ;
          GET VConditn
        READ
```

The data from the variables is displayed in a data-entry form and can be amended by the user.

```
        UPDATE Property
        SET HouseNum = VHouse, Street = VStreet,
        YearC = VYear, Conditn = VConditn
        WHERE CURRENT OF MyCursor;
```

The amended data is now written back to the rows.

```
    ENDIF
ENDDO
CLOSE MyCursor;
```

Finally, cursors can be used to delete rows from a table. This is achieved by extending the DELETE command in the same way as the UPDATE command. The DELETE command can then be used to remove from the table the last row which was retrieved by the FETCH command. For example:

```
DELETE FROM Property
WHERE CURRENT OF MyCursor;
```

This method is used in the following program. This is the same update program as above, but enhanced to cater for deletions.

Figure 11.3 shows the data-entry form extended to include a field in which the user can indicate if the relevant row is to be deleted. The field is pre-set to N. If the user overtypes this with Y, the program will delete the row.

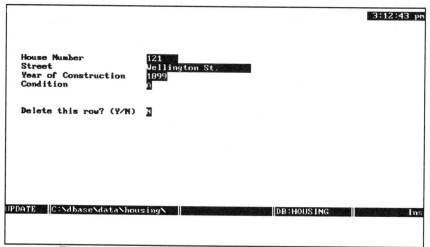

Fig. 11.3 Data-entry screen with option to delete the row.

```
* Update4.Prs
* Prompts for a house number and street, then presents
* the corresponding rows in a form which the user can
* update. Also gives the option of deleting the row
CLEAR
```

```
STORE SPACE(6) TO VHouse
STORE SPACE(20) TO VStreet
@ 5,3 SAY 'House Number          ' GET VHouse
@ 6,3 SAY 'Street                ' GET VStreet
READ
STORE TRIM(VStreet) + '*' TO VStreet
CLEAR
* Create a cursor for the row to be altered
DECLARE  MyCursor CURSOR
FOR SELECT  HouseNum, Street, YearC, Conditn
FROM Property
WHERE  Street LIKE VStreet
AND HouseNum = VHouse
FOR UPDATE OF HouseNum, Street, YearC, Conditn;
OPEN MyCursor;
IF SQLCNT = 0
    WAIT 'Not found. Press any key to proceed.'
    STORE .F. TO Ok
ELSE
    STORE .T. TO Ok
ENDIF
* The following will be executed for each row in the
* cursor
DO WHILE Ok
    * Copies values from the rows to variables
    FETCH MyCursor
     INTO VHouse, VStreet, VYear VConditn;
    IF SQLCODE <> 0
        STORE .F. TO Ok
    ELSE
       CLEAR
       * Use the variables to create a form for
       * updating
        STORE 'N' TO ToDelete
        @ 5,3 SAY 'House Number          ' GET VHouse
        @ 6,3 SAY 'Street                ' GET VStreet
        @ 7,3 SAY 'Year of Construction  ' GET VYear;
          PICTURE '####'
        @ 8,3 SAY 'Condition             ' ;
          GET VConditn
        @ 11,3 SAY 'Delete this row? (Y/N) ' ;
          GET ToDelete
        READ
```

145

```
IF UPPER(ToDelete) = 'N'
      * The updated row is to be written back
      UPDATE Property
      SET HouseNum = VHouse, Street = VStreet,
      YearC = VYear, Conditn = VConditn
      WHERE CURRENT OF MyCursor;
ELSE
      * The row is to be deleted
      DELETE FROM Property
      WHERE CURRENT OF MyCursor;
ENDIF
   ENDIF
ENDDO
CLOSE MyCursor;
```

11.4.2 Summary of cursors

The following is a summary of a program which uses a cursor and does not involve updating the table:

```
DECLARE cursor name CURSOR
FOR SELECT columns
FROM table name
WHERE condition;
   .
   .
OPEN cursor name;
DO WHILE condition
   IF SLQCODE <> 0
        finish the loop
   ELSE
        FETCH cursor name INTO variables;
   ENDIF
ENDDO
CLOSE cursor name;
```

The following is a summary of a program which uses a cursor and which permits the table to be updated:

```
DECLARE cursor name CURSOR
FOR SELECT columns
FROM table name
WHERE condition
FOR UPDATE OF columns;
```

146

```
OPEN cursor name;
DO WHILE condition
    IF SLQCODE <> 0
        finish the loop
    ELSE
        FETCH cursor name INTO variables;
        .
        .
        UPDATE table name
        SET column 1 = value 1, ...
        WHERE CURRENT OF cursor name;
        .
        .
        DELETE FROM table name
        WHERE CURRENT OF cursor name;
        .
        .

    ENDIF
ENDDO
.
.
CLOSE cursor name;
```

11.5 An improved data-entry program

The data-entry program in Section 11.2 works well. However, the user does have the responsibility of ensuring that each property has a unique property number. A better possibility would be to arrange for the computer to generate the identifying property number automatically. This can be achieved by looking at the number of the previously entered property and incrementing it by one. This implies that, after a property has been entered, its number must be saved in some way. We can do this by setting up a separate table.

We will call this table HelpTab. Although its only purpose is to store a single value, it consists of two columns. The first is used to identify the value. In this case, it contains the word 'Previous', to indicate that the value is used to determine the number of the previous property. The second column contains the actual value which we wish to store, that is, the relevant property number. We use one column to identify the other in this way in order to provide a safeguard. Without this, any blank row which might creep into the table could cause the program to fail.

The following SQL instructions are used to create HelpTab and to insert the data:

147

```
CREATE TABLE HelpTab
(H_Type CHAR(8), H_Number INTEGER);
INSERT INTO HelpTab
VALUES ('Previous', 0);
```

and this one is used to retrieve the stored value:

```
SELECT H_Number
FROM HelpTab
WHERE H_Type = 'Previous';
```

The following data-entry program uses this table to generate the property numbers automatically.

```
* Input1.Prs
* Improved version; generates PropNum automatically.
* The number of the previously-entered property is in
* HelpTab, in the H_Number column, in a row whose
* H_Type column contains 'Previous'.
* Start by retrieving the previous record's PropNum
SELECT H_Number
INTO NextNumber
FROM HelpTab
WHERE H_Type = 'Previous';
STORE NextNumber + 1 TO VPropNum
STORE SPACE(6) TO VHouse
STORE SPACE(20) TO VStreet
STORE 0 TO VYear
STORE ' ' TO VConditn
CLEAR
@ 5,3 SAY 'House Number           ' GET VHouse
@ 6,3 SAY 'Street                 ' GET VStreet
@ 7,3 SAY 'Year of Construction   ' GET VYear ;
   PICTURE '####'
@ 8,3 SAY 'Condition              ' GET VConditn
READ
INSERT INTO Property
VALUES(VPropNum,VHouse,VStreet,VYear,VConditn);
* Now store the PropNum of the record just entered
UPDATE HelpTab
SET H_Number = VPropNum
WHERE H_Sort = 'Previous';
```

148

11.6 Procedures

Every 'real' programming language gives programmers some way of constructing programs out of small building blocks called **modules**. In dBASE terminology, these modules are called **procedures**.

A procedure always begins with the keyword PROCEDURE, immediately followed by the procedure's name. This is followed by the actual commands which make up the procedure. The procedure is terminated by a RETURN command. All the program's procedures may be held in a single .PRS file.

To execute (or **call**) a procedure, you issue a command whose general form is:

```
DO procedure name
```

In addition to the procedures, every program must have a **main program**. This usually defines the program's overall structure, while calling individual procedures to handle the more detailed work. Procedures may themselves call **lower-level** procedures.

Here is a very simple example of a main program which calls two procedures:

```
* Juliet.Prs

* Begin main program
DO RomeoPrc
DO RomeoPrc
DO ArtPrc
DO RomeoPrc
RETURN
* --------
PROCEDURE RomeoPrc
? 'Romeo'
RETURN
* --------
PROCEDURE ArtPrc
? 'Wherefore art thou,'
RETURN
```

The output from this program would be

```
Romeo
Romeo
```

```
Wherefore art thou,
Romeo
```

Procedures are often stored in the same program file as the main program. The main program must always appear first in the file.

Recursion (a technique in which procedures call themselves) is strongly discouraged in dBASE, as it is likely to lead to programs going badly wrong. If you need to perform an operation several times, you should code it in the form of a DO WHILE/ENDDO loop.

The use of procedures promotes a style of working known as **structured programming**. This is essentially a 'divide-and-conquer' approach to problem-solving. By allowing big problems (the entire program) to be broken into a number of smaller sub-problems (the individual procedures), it encourages the programmer to concentrate on one aspect of the problem at a time. Without structured programming, a large application would become just a complex and tangled sequence of instructions which could be impossible to read or debug.

Structured programming implies a **top-down** method of working. The programmer starts with the big picture: the overall structure of the program. He relegates each of the main areas of detail to a lower-level procedure. Once the main structure of the program has been established, he turns his attention to the first of the detailed procedures. This procedure might in turn have an overall structure, with the details being further relegated to still lower levels. The programmer proceeds in this way until he reaches a level of detail at which the remaining problems are easily solved.

An alternative approach is the **bottom-up** method. Here, the programmer starts by writing small, simple procedures at the lowest level. He then combines these to form slightly more complex procedures, which are in turn combined to form procedures which are more complex still.

In practice, most applications are developed using a combination of top-down and bottom-up methods.

11.7 A complete application

To end this chapter, we will take a look at a complete program. This program provides all the basic functions which a user would need in order to maintain the Property table and perform simple queries, all in a user-friendly manner. We will start by splitting up the problem into a number of sub-problems, each of which represents one of the main functions of the program:

A complete application

Input new records
Enquiries
Amending and deleting records
Obtaining a summary
Creating a menu to enable the user to make choices.

The solutions to the first four sub-problems have been presented earlier in the chapter. It only remains to deal with the problem of the user's menu.

A menu system is little more than a loop. This loop does three things: displays text to prompt the user for a choice; accepts the choice from the user and stores it in a variable; and calls procedures to execute the choices. This last part of the loop is usually done from within a CASE construction.

The structure of the program can be summarised in Fig. 11.4. The program itself appears below.

```
* Complete.Prs
* A complete but simple application for maintaining
* and searching a single table

* Main program
SET TALK OFF
START DATABASE Housing;
STORE .T. TO Proceed
DO WHILE Proceed
    CLEAR
    @ 4,4   SAY 'PROPERTY INFORMATION SYSTEM'
    @ 6,4   SAY 'E = Enquiries'
    @ 7,4   SAY 'S = Summary'
    @ 8,4   SAY 'N = New properties'
    @ 9,4   SAY 'U = Update properties'
    @ 11,4 SAY 'X = Exit the program'
    ?
    WAIT '    What is your choice: ' TO Choice
    STORE UPPER(Choice) TO Choice
    DO CASE
        CASE Choice = 'E'
            DO Enquire
        CASE Choice = 'S'
            DO Summary
        CASE Choice = 'N'
            DO Input
```

151

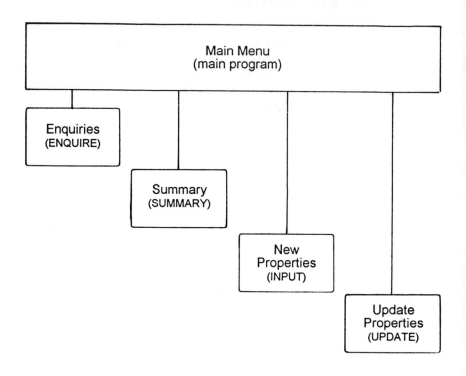

Fig. 11.4 The structure of the application.

```
          CASE Choice = 'U'
               DO Update
          CASE Choice = 'X'
               STORE .F. TO Proceed
     ENDCASE
ENDDO
SET TALK ON
RETURN
*--------
```

152

```
PROCEDURE Enquire
* Prompts the user for the house and street, then
* makes a selection based on the entered values
CLEAR
STORE SPACE(6) TO VHouse
STORE SPACE(20) TO VStreet
CLEAR
@ 5,3 SAY 'House Number          ' GET VHouse
@ 6,3 SAY 'Street                ' GET VStreet
READ
* To avoid having to force the user to enter a complete
* street name, we will append an asterisk to it after
* first removing any trailing spaces. This will allow
* us to search on a partial name, using LIKE with a
* wildcard.
STORE TRIM(VStreet) + '*' TO VStreet
CLEAR
SELECT * FROM Property
WHERE HouseNum = VHouse
AND Street LIKE VStreet;
IF SQLCNT = 0
    ? 'No property found'
ENDIF
WAIT 'Press any key to continue'
RETURN
*-------
PROCEDURE Summary
CLEAR
  SELECT * FROM Property
  ORDER BY HouseNum, Street;
WAIT 'Press any key to continue'
RETURN
*-------
PROCEDURE Input
CLEAR
* The number of the previously entered property is in
* the help table, in the H_Number column, in a row
* whose H_Type column contains 'Previous'.

* Start by retrieving the previous record's PropNum
SELECT H_Number
INTO NextNumber
FROM HelpTab
```

153

```
WHERE H_Type = 'Previous';
STORE NextNumber + 1 TO VPropNum
STORE SPACE(6) TO VHouse
STORE SPACE(20) TO VStreet
STORE 0 TO VYear
STORE ' ' TO VConditn
CLEAR
@ 5,3 SAY 'House Number              ' GET VHouse
@ 6,3 SAY 'Street                    ' GET VStreet
@ 7,3 SAY 'Year of Construction    ' GET VYear ;
  PICTURE '####'
@ 8,3 SAY 'Condition                ' ;
  GET VConditn
READ
INSERT INTO Property
VALUES(VPropNum,VHouse,VStreet,VYear,VConditn);
* Now store the PropNum of the record just entered
UPDATE HelpTab
SET H_Number = VPropNum
WHERE H_Sort = 'Previous';
RETURN
*-------
PROCEDURE Update
* Prompts for a house number and street, then presents
* the corresponding rows in a form which the user can
* update. Also gives the option of deleting the row
CLEAR
STORE SPACE(6) TO VHouse
STORE SPACE(20) TO VStreet
CLEAR
@ 5,3 SAY 'House Number              ' GET VHouse
@ 6,3 SAY 'Street                    ' GET VStreet
READ
STORE TRIM(VStreet) + '*' TO VStreet
CLEAR
* Create a cursor for the row to be altered
DECLARE  MyCursor CURSOR
FOR SELECT  HouseNum, Street, YearC, Conditn
FROM Property
WHERE  Street LIKE VStreet
AND HouseNum = VHouse
FOR UPDATE OF HouseNum, Street, YearC, Conditn;
OPEN MyCursor;
```

154

```
IF SQLCNT = 0
    WAIT 'Not found. Press any key to proceed.'
    STORE .F. TO Ok
ELSE
    STORE .T. TO Ok
ENDIF
* The following will be executed for each row in the
* cursor
DO WHILE Ok
    * Copies values from the rows to variables
    FETCH MyCursor
    INTO VHouse, VStreet, VYear VConditn;
    IF SQLCODE <> 0
        STORE .F. TO Ok
    ELSE
      CLEAR
      * Use the variables to create a form for
      * updating
      STORE 'N' TO ToDelete
      @ 5,3 SAY 'House Number          ' GET VHouse
      @ 6,3 SAY 'Street                ' GET VStreet
      @ 7,3 SAY 'Year of Construction  ' GET VYear ;
          PICTURE '####'
      @ 8,3 SAY 'Condition             ' ;
        GET VConditn
      @ 11,3 SAY 'Delete this row? (Y/N) ' ;
        GET ToDelete
      READ
      IF UPPER(ToDelete) = 'N'
          * The updated row is to be written back
          UPDATE Property
          SET HouseNum = VHouse, Street = VStreet,
          YearC = VYear, Conditn = VConditn
          WHERE CURRENT OF MyCursor;
      ELSE
          * The row is to be deleted
          DELETE FROM Property
          WHERE CURRENT OF MyCursor;
      ENDIF
    ENDIF
ENDDO
CLOSE MyCursor;
RETURN
```

CHAPTER TWELVE

A complete application

12.1 Introduction

In this chapter, we will look at a complete application in depth. The application is based on our sample Housing database, and is intended to provide information for research into the housing market. In planning the application, we will pay close attention to the principles of referential integrity.

Clearly, one of the most important steps in developing any application is to define the structure of the database. But before we can do even that, we must decide exactly what the application is required to do.

12.2 The requirements

It is an implicit requirement that the application must observe the principles of referential integrity. We have already taken this requirement into account when designing the database, in particular by specifying that each property must have a unique identifying number. However, this in itself does not guarantee integrity, for the following reasons:

(a)   There is nothing to prevent the user from using the same property number for more than one property.

(b)   Integrity could be lost if the user entered a transaction (in this case, details of a property sale) in respect of a property which was not present in the Property table.

All application programs have to find a way of guarding against these types of errors. The program which appears in Section 11.7, for example, deals with the first of these problems by generating unique property numbers automatically (in the Input procedure) and by not providing the user with any way of altering the generated numbers.

156

The other requirements of the program depend on the needs and goals of the users. In our example, we will assume that the users have the following aims:

(a) To retrieve all information relating to a specific address.
(b) To retrieve all information relating to a particular person or company.
(c) To retrieve information about properties where the exact address is not known. This can be achieved by listing all the properties in a given street or in the entire database.
(d) To determine the profits of each property company.

Figure 12.1 shows the structure of the application in diagrammatic form.

12.3 The input

The design of the Housing database follows a well-tried pattern. It has a main table (Properties) and a detail table (Sales). For each row in the main table, there is a variable number of rows in the detail table.

12.3.1. Inputting property records

Since the design relies on the presence of a unique identifying number in the main table, we need a mechanism to prevent duplicate values for this number from entering the table. Our application will therefore include a similar input procedure to the one shown in Section 11.7. It will also have an additional feature: it will prevent blank addresses from being entered.

```
PROCEDURE NewProp
* Input procedure for a new property
CLEAR
* The number of the previously entered property is in
* the help table, in the H_Number column, in a row
* whose H_Type column contains 'Previous'.

* Start by retrieving the previous record's PropNum
SELECT H_Number
INTO NextNumber
FROM HelpTab
WHERE H_Type = 'Previous';
STORE NextNumber + 1 TO VPropNum
STORE SPACE(6) TO VHouse
STORE SPACE(20) TO VStreet
```

157

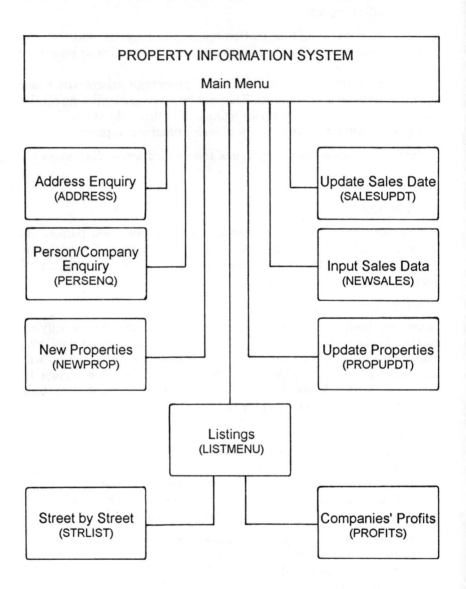

Fig. 12.1 Diagrammatic representation of the sample application.

```
STORE 0 TO VYear
STORE ' ' TO VConditn
CLEAR
@ 5,3 SAY 'House Number            ' GET VHouse
@ 6,3 SAY 'Street                  ' GET VStreet
@ 7,3 SAY 'Year of Construction    ' GET VYear ;
   PICTURE '####'
@8,3 SAY 'Condition                ' GET VConditn
READ
IF LEN(TRIM(VHouse)) = 0 .OR. LEN(TRIM(VStreet)) = 0
    ? 'Incomplete address. Record not saved.'
    WAIT 'Press any key to continue'
ELSE
    INSERT INTO Property
    VALUES (VPropNum, VHouse, VStreet,
    VYear, VConditn);
    * Now store the PropNum of the record just entered
    UPDATE HelpTab
    SET H_Number = VPropNum
    WHERE H_Sort = 'Previous';
ENDIF
RETURN
```

12.3.2 Inputting sales records

Our program will have a separate procedure for entering new sales records. In order to help maintain referential integrity, this procedure performs a number of checks on the addresses typed in by the user.

First, the procedure must ensure that the property to which the sales record relates is already present in the Property table. It therefore starts by inviting the user to type the house number and street name. It then checks these details against the Property table. If the address is not present, it advises the user and refrains from accepting any further details for the sale. The user would then have to enter the relevant information into the Property table before being able to proceed with the entry of the sale.

At the same time, the procedure checks that a given address is not present more than once in the Property table. If the user was allowed to enter a sale in respect of a duplicate property number, the program would almost certainly go wrong. Instead, the procedure declines to accept the sale until the user has deleted the superfluous records from the Property table.

Only if the address in the sales record occurs exactly once in the

Property table will the procedure allow the full sales data to be entered. The procedure invites the user to enter the date, price, buyer and seller. It obtains the property number from the Property table (in the record containing the address which the user just typed in). These fields then form the new row which is to be added to the Sales table.

Here is the entire sales input procedure:

```
PROCEDURE NewSales
* Input procedure for a sales transaction. Checks the
* address against the Property table and retrieves the
* corresponding property number.
STORE SPACE(6) TO VHouse
STORE SPACE(20) TO VStreet
CLEAR
@ 5,3 SAY 'House Number          ' GET VHouse
@ 6,3 SAY 'Street                ' GET VStreet
READ
STORE TRIM(VStreet) + '*' TO VStreet
STORE 0 TO Addr_Count
SELECT COUNT(*)
INTO Addr_Count
FROM Property
WHERE HouseNum = VHouse AND Street LIKE VStreet;
IF Addr_Count = 0
    ? 'Property is not present in the database'
    WAIT 'You must first enter the property details'
ENDIF
If Addr_Count > 1
    ? 'Property occurs more than once in the database'
    WAIT 'You must first remove the surplus details'
ENDIF
IF Addr_Count = 1
    SELECT PropNum INTO VPropNum FROM Property
    WHERE HouseNum = VHouse AND Street LIKE VStreet;
    STORE {00/00/00} TO VDate
    STORE 0 TO VPrice
    STORE SPACE(20) TO VBuyer
    STORE SPACE(20) TO VSeller
    @ 9,3  SAY 'Date             ' GET VDate
    @ 10,3 SAY 'Price            ' GET VPrice;
       PICTURE '999999'
    @ 11,3 SAY 'Buyer            ' GET VBuyer
```

160

```
@ 12,3 SAY 'Seller                    ' GET VSeller
READ
INSERT INTO Sales
VALUES (VPropNum, VDate, VPrice, VSeller);
ENDIF
RETURN
```

Looking at this procedure in detail:

```
STORE SPACE(6) TO VHouse
STORE SPACE(20) TO VStreet
CLEAR
@ 5,3 SAY 'House Number          ' GET VHouse
@ 6,3 SAY 'Street                ' GET VStreet
READ
STORE TRIM(VStreet) + '*' TO VStreet
```

These lines deal with the entry of the address.

```
STORE 0 TO Addr_Count
SELECT COUNT(*)
INTO Addr_Count
FROM Property
WHERE HouseNum = VHouse AND Street LIKE VStreet;
```

Here, we find out how many times the address occurs in the Property table. Note that the Addr_Count variable must be initialised before the SELECT command is executed. This is because the SELECT does not create the variable if no rows were returned.

```
IF Addr_Count = 0
    ? 'Property is not present in the database'
    WAIT 'You must first enter the property details'
ENDIF
If Addr_Count > 1
    ? 'Property occurs more than once in the database'
    WAIT 'You must first remove the surplus details'
ENDIF
```

These commands check for the two possible errors and advise the user accordingly.

```
IF Addr_Count = 1
```

161

```
SELECT PropNum INTO VPropNum FROM Property
WHERE HouseNum = VHouse AND Street LIKE VStreet;
```

This retrieves the property number from the Property table.

```
STORE {00/00/00} TO VDate
STORE 0 TO VPrice
STORE SPACE(20) TO VBuyer
STORE SPACE(20) TO VSeller
@ 9,3  SAY 'Date              ' GET VDate
@ 10,3 SAY 'Price             ' GET VPrice ;
   PICTURE '999999'
@ 11,3 SAY 'Buyer             ' GET VBuyer
@ 12,3 SAY 'Seller            ' GET VSeller
READ
```

The remaining property details are obtained from the user.

```
INSERT INTO Sales
   VALUES (VPropNum, VDate, VPrice, VSeller);
ENDIF
```

Finally, the new row is added to the Sales table.

12.4 Updating

12.4.1 Updating the Property table

As far as the main table is concerned, the update procedure is similar
to the one shown in Section 11.7. The requirement to maintain
integrity is met partly by the fact that the data-entry form does not
have a field for property number. However, integrity is still not
watertight because the procedure does not prevent the deletion of a
property for which sales records exist.

```
PROCEDURE PropUpdt
* Update procedure for properties
STORE SPACE(6) TO VHouse
STORE SPACE(20) TO VStreet
CLEAR
@ 5,3 SAY 'House Number       ' GET VHouse
@ 6,3 SAY 'Street             ' GET VStreet
READ
```

```
STORE TRIM(VStreet) + '*' TO VStreet
CLEAR
* Create a cursor for the row to be altered
DECLARE MyCursor CURSOR
FOR SELECT  HouseNum, Street, YearC, Conditn
FROM Property
WHERE  Street LIKE VStreet
AND HouseNum = VHouse
FOR UPDATE OF HouseNum, Street, YearC, Conditn;
OPEN MyCursor;
IF SQLCNT = 0
    WAIT 'Not found. Press any key to proceed.'
    STORE .F. TO Ok
ELSE
    STORE .T. TO Ok
ENDIF
* The following will be executed for each row in the
* cursor
DO WHILE Ok
    * Copies values from the rows to variables
    FETCH MyCursor
    INTO VHouse, VStreet, VYear VConditn;
    IF SQLCODE <> 0
        STORE .F. TO Ok
    ELSE
      CLEAR
      * Use the variables to create a form for
      * updating
       STORE 'N' TO ToDelete
       @ 5,3 SAY 'House Number          ' GET VHouse
       @ 6,3 SAY 'Street                ' GET VStreet
       @ 7,3 SAY 'Year of Construction  ' GET VYear ;
         PICTURE '####'
       @ 8,3 SAY 'Condition             ' ;
         GET VConditn
       @ 11,3 SAY 'Delete this row? (Y/N) ' ;
         GET ToDelete
      READ
      IF UPPER(ToDelete) = 'N'
          * The updated row is to be written back
          UPDATE Property
          SET HouseNum = VHouse, Street = VStreet,
          YearC = VYear, Conditn = VConditn
```

163

```
            WHERE CURRENT OF MyCursor;
        ELSE
            * The row is to be deleted
            DELETE FROM Property
            WHERE CURRENT OF MyCursor;
        ENDIF
    ENDIF
ENDDO
CLOSE MyCursor;
RETURN
```

12.4.2 Updating the Sales table

The procedure for amending the Sales table is a little more complicated than for the Property table. Here the user enters a house number and street. The procedure obtains the corresponding property number from the Property table. This property number is then used to create a cursor containing the rows to be amended.

```
PROCEDURE SaleUpdt
* Update procedure for sales
STORE SPACE(6) TO VHouse
STORE SPACE(20) TO VStreet
CLEAR
@ 5,3 SAY 'House Number            ' GET VHouse
@ 6,3 SAY 'Street                  ' GET VStreet
READ
STORE TRIM(VStreet) + '*' TO VStreet
STORE 0 TO Addr_Count
SELECT COUNT(*)
INTO Addr_Count
FROM Property
WHERE HouseNum = VHouse AND Street LIKE VStreet;
IF Addr_Count = 0
    ? 'Property is not present in the database'
    WAIT 'You must first enter the property details'
ENDIF
If Addr_Count > 1
    ? 'Property occurs more than once in the database'
    WAIT 'You must first remove the surplus details'
ENDIF
IF Addr_Count = 1
    SELECT PropNum INTO VPropNum FROM Property
    WHERE HouseNum = VHouse AND Street LIKE VStreet;
```

164

```
* Create a cursor with the rows to be altered
DECLARE UpdtCur CURSOR
FOR SELECT Date, Price, Buyer, Seller
FROM Sales WHERE PropNum = VPropNum
FOR UPDATE OF Date, Price, Buyer, Seller;
OPEN UpdtCur;
IF SQLCNT = 0
    WAIT 'Sales data not found. Press any key'
ENDIF
* The following loop is executed for each cursor
* row
STORE .T. TO Ok
DO WHILE Ok
    * Copy values from the cursor row to variables
    FETCH UpdtCur
    INTO VDate, VPrice, VBuyer, VSeller;
    * SQLCODE will be zero until there are no more
    * rows in the cursor, or there is a problem
    * with the FETCH. This fact can be used to
    * decide when to end the loop.
    IF SQLCODE <> 0
        STORE .F. TO Ok
    ELSE
        CLEAR
        * Allow user to update the variables
        STORE 'N' TO ToDelete
        @ 9,3  SAY 'Date                   ' ;
          GET VDate
        @ 10,3 SAY 'Price                  ' ;
          GET VPrice PICTURE '999999'
        @ 11,3 SAY 'Buyer                  ' ;
          GET VBuyer
        @ 12,3 SAY 'Seller                 ' ;
          GET VSeller
        @ 13,3 SAY 'Delete this row? (Y/N) ' ;
          GET ToDelete
        READ
        IF UPPER(ToDelete) = 'N'
            * The updated row is to be written back
            UPDATE Sales
            SET Date = VDate, Price = VPrice,
            Buyer = VBuyer, Seller = VSeller
            WHERE CURRENT OF UpdtCur;
```

165

```
          ELSE
                * The row is to be deleted
                DELETE FROM Sales
                WHERE CURRENT OF UpdtCur;
             ENDIF
          ENDIF
       ENDDO
       CLOSE UpdtCur;
    ENDIF
    RETURN
```

12.5 Enquiries

Our application has two enquiry procedures, one for addresses and one for people and companies. In both cases, joins are used to combine the data from the two tables and to present an overall view of the information.

12.5.1 Enquiries on addresses

To help make the output more readable, this procedure displays the property data first, then the sales data.

```
PROCEDURE AddrEnq
* Prompt the user for a house number and a street,
* and display data based on the combination of the two.
CLEAR
STORE SPACE(6) TO VHouse
STORE SPACE(20) TO VStreet
READ
STORE TRIM(VStreet) + '*' TO VStreet
CLEAR
SELECT * FROM Property
WHERE HouseNum = VHouse
AND Street LIKE VStreet;
? 'Transactions'
SELECT Date, Price, Buyer, Seller
FROM Property, Sales
WHERE HouseNum = VHouse
AND Street LIKE VStreet
AND Property.PropNum = Sales.PropNum;
IF SQLCNT = 0
    ? 'No sales data found.'
ENDIF
```

166

```
WAIT 'Press any key to continue.'
RETURN
```

12.5.2 Enquiries on people and companies

In the other enquiry procedure, the user types the name of a person or firm. The procedure displays all the sales data for which the specified person is either the buyer or seller, along with the corresponding property details.

```
PROCEDURE PersEnq
* Prompt the user for a person or company and
* display all relevant data
STORE SPACE(20) TO Person
CLEAR
@ 5,3 SAY 'Name of person or firm: ' GET Person
READ
STORE TRIM(Person) + '*' TO Person
CLEAR
SELECT HouseNum, Street, Buyer, Date, Price, Seller
FROM Property, Sales
WHERE  (Buyer LIKE Person OR Seller LIKE Person)
AND Property.PropNum = Sales.PropNum;
IF SQLCNT = 0
    ? 'No data found'
ENDIF
WAIT 'Press any key to continue.'
RETURN
```

12.6 Listings

12.6.1 Listing by street

One of the requirements of the application is to produce a listing of all properties in a given street. This can be done as follows:

```
PROCEDURE StrList
* Street-by-street listing
STORE SPACE(20) TO VStreet
CLEAR
@ 5,3 SAY 'Street     ' GET VStreet
@ 7,3 SAY 'To see ALL streets, leave the field empty'
READ
STORE TRIM(VStreet) + '*' TO VStreet
```

167

```
CLEAR
SELECT * FROM Property
WHERE Street LIKE VStreet
ORDER BY HouseNum, Street;
WAIT 'Press any key to continue.'
CLEAR
? 'Transactions'
SELECT Date, Price, Buyer, Seller
FROM Property, Sales
WHERE Street LIKE VStreet
AND Property.PropNum = Sales.PropNum
ORDER BY HouseNum, Street;
IF SQLCNT = 0
    ? 'No data found.'
ENDIF
WAIT 'Press any key to continue.'
RETURN
```

If the user left the street empty, the VStreet variable would contain just an asterisk. This would cause all streets to be found.

12.6.2 Listing of profits

The requirements also included a means to determine each company's profits. This can be done as follows (see also Section 6.3).

```
PROCEDURE Profits
* Determine the profits for company
CLEAR
SELECT SUM(sell.Price - buy.Price), buy.Buyer
FROM Sales buy, Sales sell
WHERE buy.PropNum = sell.PropNum
AND buy.Buyer = sell.Seller
GROUP BY buy.Buyer;
WAIT 'Press any key to continue.'
RETURN
```

12.7 The finished program

Most of the sections of the program which we have seen so far in this chapter are separate procedures. These procedures are called by a top-level menu. This menu constitutes the main program. It also calls a sub-menu which allows the user to select one of the two types of listing. The sub-menu in turn calls the two listing procedures.

The finished program

The main program includes these commands:

```
SET TALK OFF
```

and

```
SET PAUSE ON
```

The first of these commands suppresses certain messages which dBASE IV would otherwise place on the screen. If this was not done, the messages would interfere with the display and prevent the program from interacting properly with the user.

The second of the commands is used to prevent the output from a SELECT command from scrolling off the screen before the user could read it. Once SET PAUSE ON has been issued, the program will wait for the user to press a key whenever the screen is filled up.

```
* Housing.Prs
* Property Information System

* Main program
SET TALK OFF
START DATABASE Housing;
SET PAUSE ON
STORE .T. TO More
DO WHILE More
    CLEAR
    @ 4,4  SAY 'PROPERTY INFORMATION SYSTEM'
    @ 6,4  SAY 'A = Address enquiry'
    @ 7,4  SAY 'P = Person/company enquiry'
    @ 8,4  SAY 'L = Listings'
    @ 9,4  SAY 'N = New properties'
    @ 10,4 SAY 'U = Update properties'
    @ 11,4 SAY 'I = Input sales data'
    @ 12,4 SAY 'S = Update sales data'
    @ 13,4 SAY 'X = Exit the program'
    ?
    WAIT '    What is your choice? ' TO MainChoice
    STORE UPPER(MainChoice) TO
    DO CASE
        CASE MainChoice = 'A'
            DO AddrEnq
        CASE MainChoice = 'P'
```

169

```
                DO PersEnq
        CASE MainChoice = 'L'
                DO ListMenu
        CASE MainChoice = 'N'
                DO NewProp
        CASE MainChoice = 'U'
                DO PropUpdt
        CASE MainChoice = 'I'
                DO NewSales
        CASE MainChoice = 'S'
                DO SaleUpdt
        CASE MainChoice = 'X'
                STORE .F. TO More
     ENDCASE
ENDDO
SET TALK ON
RETURN
* End of main program


* Subsidiary procedures
PROCEDURE NewProp
   .
   .
   .
RETURN
* --------
PROCEDURE NewSales
   .
   .
   .
RETURN
* -------
PROCEDURE PropUpdt
   .
   .
   .
RETURN
* ------
PROCEDURE SaleUpdt
   .
   .
   .
RETURN
```

```
* --------
PROCEDURE AddrEnq
.
.
.
RETURN
* -------
PROCEDURE PersEnq
.
.
.
RETURN
* -------
PROCEDURE ListMenu
* Sub-menu for choosing a listing
CLEAR
@ 4,4 SAY 'LISTINGS'
@ 6,4 SAY '1 = Street-by-street listing'
@ 7,4 SAY "2 = Companies' profits"
@ 8,4 SAY '0 = Return to main menu'
?
WAIT '    What is your choice? ' TO SubChoice
DO CASE
    CASE SubChoice = '1'
        DO StrList
    CASE SubChoice = '2'
        DO Profits
ENDCASE
RETURN
* ------
PROCEDURE StrList
.
.
.
RETURN
* -----
PROCEDURE Profits
.
.
.
RETURN
* End of program
```

CHAPTER THIRTEEN

Database miscellany

13.1 Introduction

In this chapter, we will take a brief look at some further aspects of
dBASE IV/SQL. Although strictly speaking these do not come under
the heading of database management, it would be impossible to
conclude our study without at least acknowledging their existence.

We will cover the following topics:

(a)   More advanced features of the dBASE language;
(b)   Data import and export;
(c)   Reports and graphics;
(d)   Multi-user features, including client-server architecture;
(e)   Security aspects;
(f)   Transaction processing.

These are all fairly deep topics, and we can do no more than
provide a quick introduction to them. A more thorough treatment
would be well beyond the scope of this book. The purpose of this
chapter is to give you a taste of what is possible in the hope that you
will wish to explore some or all of the subjects further. If you decide
to do so, you are strongly recommended to study the documentation
which comes with the dBASE IV package.

13.2 Going further with the dBASE language

The dBASE IV programming language is so extensive that it would
be impossible – much less advisable – to try to describe all its
features in an introductory work like this. The language includes 128
built-in functions (including a number of specialised statistical and
financial functions), 145 separate commands, a further 77 SET
commands (used for altering the behaviour of dBASE in various
ways) and much more. The aim of this section is to give an overview
of what is possible with the language, without going into details.

172

13.2.1 Manipulating data

A high proportion of those 145 commands are concerned with data manipulation, including searching for data and updating databases. These data-handling commands cannot be used in SQL mode or included in programs which are held in .PRS files (the APPEND, BROWSE and EDIT commands are exceptions).

As mentioned earlier, dBASE IV supports two modes: SQL mode (used by .PRS programs) and non-SQL mode (also called dBASE mode). Programs intended to run in non-SQL mode are held in files which have the extension .PRG. You cannot place SQL commands in .PRG files, although there is nothing stopping a .PRG program from calling a .PRS program with a DO command.

13.2.2 Arrays

As well as variables, the dBASE language supports **arrays**. You can think of an array as a variable which contains a number of separate 'compartments' (called **elements**). Each element can hold a separate value.

13.2.3 Parameters

When calling a procedure, it is possible to pass it one or more specific values for it to work with. These values are called **parameters**.

In the examples earlier in this book, each procedure is self-contained. No information is passed from one procedure to another, or between the procedure and the main program. Up to a point, data can be shared among procedures simply by storing the appropriate values in ordinary variables. However, this is not always practical, mainly because of dBASE's **scoping rules**. These say, among other things, that a variable created in one procedure is not accessible in a higher-level procedure.

Parameters, on the other hand, are specifically designed for passing values between procedures. The calling procedure passes parameters to a lower-level procedure by means of the WITH clause in the DO command. The called procedure issues a PARAMETERS command to identify the parameters. It can then treat the parameters just like any other variables. The variables do not have to have the same names as in the calling program. They will, however, have the same value initially.

The following example shows how it works:

```
* Program to calculate squares
STORE 2 TO Target
DO Square WITH Target
```

```
? Target
RETURN


PROCEDURE Square
PARAMETERS Numb
STORE Numb * Numb TO Numb
RETURN
```

The calling program will display 4.

A less elegant method of sharing information among procedures is to declare **public** variables. These are variables which are accessible to every procedure in the program.

13.2.4 Memo fields

The dBASE language supports an additional data type: the **memo field**. This is similar to the character type, except that it is variable in length and is not subject to the 254-character limit. Memo fields only occur in databases; there is no such thing as a memo variable. Unfortunately there is no way of using memo fields from within SQL mode.

13.2.5 Saving and retrieving variables

It is possible to save the contents of variables to a disk file. The variable can then be read back, either by the same program running at a later time, or by a different program.

13.2.6 Date arithmetic

The dBASE language allows arithmetical operations to be performed on dates. Thus it is possible to subtract one date from another, the result being the number of days between the two dates. It is also possible to add a number to a date to obtain a new date, the number again being interpreted as a number of days.

13.3 Fancy menus

Although the menus in the example programs in Chapters 11 and 12 are perfectly adequate, they are a far cry from some of the impressive menu systems which form part of a modern user interface. However, dBASE IV does support a range of interesting menu types, including sliding-bar, pop-up and pull-down menus.

In a **sliding-bar menu**, the various options are arranged in a horizontal row. By using the cursor keys, the user can slide a highlighted bar from one option to another. To select an option, you move the bar to it and press Enter.

A **pop-up menu** is similar, except that the options are arranged vertically. With both types, when the user has made the selection the menu disappears, restoring whatever was on the screen before.

A **pull-down menu** is a combination of a sliding-bar menu and a pop-up menu. When the user invokes the menu, the sliding-bar appears first. When an option on this menu is selected, a pop-up menu appears showing a choice of further options. The sliding-bar menu can be thought of as the main menu, and the pop-up menus as the sub-menus.

dBASE IV itself uses all three types of menus in its own user interface. The dBASE language therefore gives programmers the opportunity to create menus which mimic those of dBASE IV.

Creating these menus requires a number of steps, and it is not possible in this short chapter to explain these in detail. But to give you a flavour of the relevant commands, here is an outline of the Housing application again, this time with a new pop-up menu (see also Fig. 13.1).

```
* Housing1.Prs

* Main program
SET TALK OFF
SET PAUSE ON
DO Def_Menu
CLEAR
ACTIVATE POPUP MainMenu
SET TALK ON
RETURN
* End of main program
* --------
PROCEDURE Def_Menu
* Defines the main pop-up menu
DEFINE POPUP MainMenu FROM 4,4;
MESSAGE ;
   'Move the bar to required option and press Enter'
DEFINE BAR 1 OF MainMenu ;
   PROMPT ' PROPERTY INFORMATION SYSTEM'  SKIP[1]
DEFINE BAR 2 OF MainMenu PROMPT ' Address enquiry'
```

---

[1]The SKIP keyword indicates that the corresponding menu item appears on the screen but cannot be selected.

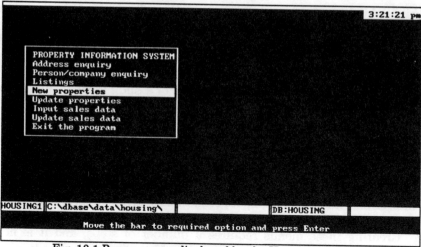

Fig. 13.1 Pop-up menu displayed by the Housing program.

```
DEFINE BAR 3 OF MainMenu ;
  PROMPT ' Person/company enquiry'
DEFINE BAR 4 OF MainMenu PROMPT ' Listings'
DEFINE BAR 5 OF MainMenu PROMPT ' New properties'
DEFINE BAR 6 OF MainMenu PROMPT ' Update properties'
DEFINE BAR 7 OF MainMenu PROMPT ' Input sales data'
DEFINE BAR 8 OF MainMenu PROMPT ' Update sales data'
DEFINE BAR 9 OF MainMenu PROMPT ' Exit the program'
ON SELECTION POPUP MainMenu DO MenuSel
RETURN
* ------------
PROCEDURE MenuSel
* Deal with the user's menu option
CLEAR
DO CASE
    CASE BAR( ) = 2
        DO AddrEnq
        CLEAR
    CASE BAR( ) = 3
        DO PersEnq
        CLEAR
    CASE BAR( ) = 4
        DO ListMenu
        CLEAR
    CASE BAR( ) = 5
        DO NewProp
```

176

```
            CLEAR
        CASE BAR( ) = 6
            DO PropUpdt
            CLEAR
        CASE BAR( ) = 7
            DO NewSales
            CLEAR
        CASE BAR( ) = 8
            DO SalesUpdt
            CLEAR
        CASE BAR( ) = 9
            DEACTIVATE POPUP
ENDCASE
RETURN
* --------
PROCEDURE NewProp
.
.
RETURN
* --------
PROCEDURE NewSales
.
.
RETURN
* --------
PROCEDURE PropUpdt
.
.
RETURN
* --------
PROCEDURE SalesUpdt
.
.
RETURN
* --------
PROCEDURE AddrEnq
.
.
RETURN
* -------
PROCEDURE PersEnq
.
.
RETURN
```

177

```
* -------
PROCEDURE ListMenu
  .
  .
RETURN
* ------
PROCEDURE StrList
  .
  .
RETURN
* ------
PROCEDURE Profits
  .
  .
RETURN
* End of program
```

A pop-up menu must be defined before it can be used. This is done by the Def_Menu procedure. At the end of the definition, the following line appears:

```
ON SELECTION POPUP MainMenu DO MenuSel
```

This command stipulates that, as soon as the user has made a selection from the menu, the MenuSel procedure will be executed.

The following command puts the pop-up menu onto the screen:

```
ACTIVATE POPUP MainMenu
```

You might have noticed that there is no DO WHILE/ENDDO loop in this program. This construction is not needed because the pop-up menu is active the whole time. As soon as the MainMenu procedure finishes, the user can once again make a selection from the menu. Control passes between the menu and the MainMenu procedure in this way, until the following command is issued:

```
DEACTIVATE POPUP
```

This happens when the user selects the option to exit the program.

In general, the application programmer can take advantage of every element of dBASE IV's own user interface. In fact, dBASE IV has two interfaces. One is the command line, which consists of a prompt against which commands can be typed. The other is the menu system, including sliding-bar and pop-up menus, as well as **windows** (a window is a distinct portion of the screen that can be manipulated in various ways; an example is dBASE IV's debugger window). It is this latter interface which is available for incorporation into application programs.

13.4 Importing data

Most database management systems have facilities for importing and exporting data, that is, for converting data from and to the formats used by other programs. dBASE IV/SQL is no exception. SQL has a LOAD DATA command which can be used to bring data into a table. Data can be imported from many different types of files, but two types are especially important: DBF and ASCII.

13.4.1 DBF data files

The DBF file format is a very widely used. It is the format which dBASE IV itself creates (as does dBASE III Plus). Various other programs, such as SPSS/PC+ and applications produced by the Clipper compiler, can create DBF files that can be read by dBASE IV.

The following command is used to transfer data from a DBF file to a dBASE IV/SQL table:

```
LOAD DATA FROM file name INTO TABLE table name;
```

13.4.2 Delimited ASCII files

ASCII files are ordinary text files which can be typed with a text-editing program (for example, the editor which in invoked by dBASE IV's MODIFY FILE). The editor must be capable of saving files without any special control or formatting codes, such as printer control codes.

In a delimited ASCII file, each record consists of a separate line. Within the records, the fields are separated by a comma.

To convert a delimited ASCII file to a dBASE IV/SQL table, you use the following command:

```
LOAD DATA FROM file name INTO TABLE table name
TYPE DELIMITED;
```

SQL's ability to import data from ASCII files provides a convenient way of entering a large number of records into a table *en bloc*. For example, to enter our sample data into the Property table, we could use a text editor to create a text file with the following lines:

179

```
1,121,Wellington St.,1899,A
2,123,Wellington St.,1899,A
3,119,Wellington St.,1899,A
4,117,Wellington St.,1899,A
5,115,Wellington St.,1899,P
6,113,Wellington St.,1898,P
7,111,Wellington St.,1898,P
8,109,Wellington St.,1898,P
9,120,Park Road,1898,P
10,122,Park Road,1898,G
```

(Be sure to press the Enter key at the end of the final line, otherwise the last record will not be imported.)

If we called this file, say, NewProps.Txt, the following command would transfer it to the Property table:

```
LOAD DATA FROM NewProps.Txt INTO TABLE Property
TYPE DELIMITED;
```

(In both these examples, the text files are assumed to be in the current directory.)

Similarly, we could enter data into the Sales table by creating the following text file:

```
1,19800225,25000,FX Properties Ltd,P Johnson
6,19811201,22500,Vista Estates Ltd,T Taylor
1,19800226,40000,Vista Estates Ltd,FX Properties Ltd
1,19800227,50000,Ballerton D.C.,Vista Estates Ltd
3,19811111,17500,Ballerton D.C.,T Zander
8,19820101,20000,Vista Estates Ltd,L Lauder
9,19820130,30000,Vista Estates Ltd,W Bendix
10,19830505,35000,FX Properties Ltd,I Stevenson
10,19830522,37500,Vista Estates Ltd,FX Properties Ltd
```

Note that dates must entered in the format YYYYMMDD.

Assuming that the file is called NewSales.Txt, we could import it into the Sales table like this:

```
LOAD DATA FROM NewSales.Txt INTO TABLE Sales
TYPE DELIMITED;
```

13.5 Exporting data

The UNLOAD DATA command is used to transfer data from an SQL table to another file type. To export to a DBF file, its general form is:

```
UNLOAD DATA TO file name FROM TABLE table name;
```

To export to other file types, you use a TYPE clause to specify the target format. For example, to export to delimited ASCII, the command would be:

```
UNLOAD DATA TO file name FROM TABLE table name
TYPE Delimited;
```

Another commonly used file type is System Data Format, or SDF. This is an ASCII file, with one record per line, but without any special characters used to separate the fields. Instead, each field occupies a fixed length. A typical SDF file looks like this:

```
 1 121 Wellington St.        1899    A
 2 123 Wellington St.        1899    A
 3 119 Wellington St.        1899    A
 4 117 Wellington St.        1899    A
 5 115 Wellington St.        1899    P
 6 113 Wellington St.        1898    P
 7 111 Wellington St.        1898    P
 8 109 Wellington St.        1898    P
 9 120 Park Road             1898    P
10 122 Park Road             1898    G
```

To create an SDF file called, say, Houses.Txt, using data from the Property table, you would issue the following command:

```
UNLOAD DATA TO Houses FROM TABLE Property TYPE SDF;
```

If the file extension is omitted from the file name in this command (as is the case here), dBASE IV/SQL adds the default extension .TXT.

SDF files can be used by a wide range of programs. It is particularly common on minicomputers and mainframes.

The UNLOAD DATA command always exports the entire contents of the specified table. If you want to export selected records only, use a SELECT command to create a temporary table (see Section 6.11), then use UNLOAD DATA to convert the temporary table to the required file format.

181

13.6 Presentation

13.6.1 Reports

One way of presenting data in an attractive format is to include it in a **report**. A report is essentially a printout which has been enhanced by the addition of titles, column headings, page numbers, total lines, etc.

dBASE IV includes a menu-driven report generator, the aim of which is to help you to design a report interactively. To design the report, you arrange fields, text, boxes, etc., on the screen. When you are happy with their appearance, you tell dBASE IV to generate a program which prints the report.

To invoke the report generator, type the following command:

```
CREATE REPORT report name
```

As an alternative to the report generator, dBASE IV provides a 'quick report' feature. To print a quick report, you press Shift-f9 from the Control Centre. The process is much easier than with the report generator, but you have less control over the layout of the report.

13.6.2 Graphs and charts

Graphs and charts provide another method of presenting data. They are particularly useful when you want to give an overall impression rather than show detailed figures. dBASE IV itself cannot produce graphs or charts, but it can pass data to specialised graphics packages, such as Harvard Graphics, Applause and Microsoft Chart.

13.7 Statistical analysis

Specialised statistical packages are available for performing complex numerical analysis of data. Most of these packages can either read .DBF files directly, or have facilities for importing them. For example, the SPSS/PC+ package can import a .DBF file via the following command:

```
TRANSLATE FROM "file name".
```

Once the data is in the package's own format, a wide range of statistical operation can be carried out on it.[1]

---

[1]Norusis (1988), p.C201 – p.C206. Version 2.0 of SPCC/PC+ does not work properly with SQL tables. Version 4.01 does not have this problem.

13.8 Systems involving more than one user

Most database management systems – and dBASE IV is no exception – allow several users to work with the same database at the same time. Exactly how they achieve this depends partly on the type of hardware available. In general, there are three approaches: a multi-user computer with terminals; a local area network that provides shared access to data files; and a client/server system.

13.8.1 Multi-user computers

A multi-user computer consists of a large central computer to which a number of terminals are attached. The central computer might be a mainframe, a minicomputer, a workstation or a PC which is running a special multi-user operating system such as Unix. The terminals might themselves be PCs which have been equipped with **terminal emulation** software. This is software which makes a PC behave like a traditional terminal.

Versions of dBASE IV are available for DEC VAX minicomputers running under VMS and ULTRIX, for Sun workstations and servers, and for 386 PCs running under SCO Unix and Interactive Unix.

The most important thing about these versions of dBASE IV is that they are almost identical to the familiar MS-Dos version, both in appearance and functionality. No special knowledge of Unix or VMS is required in order to use them. Furthermore, their file formats are completely compatible with their MS-Dos equivalents. Data files, source programs (.PRS and .PRG files) and compiled object programs (.DBO files) can all be transferred from a PC and used immediately, with no conversion necessary.[1]

13.8.2 Sharing files on a network

In a local area network, or LAN, a number of PCs are connected together with special cabling. One or more of the PCs is usually designated to act as a **file server**. A file server is essentially a PC whose hard disk can be accessed by any other PC on the network, thus providing a mechanism for sharing data. Each PC on the network is equipped with a network adapter card which enables it to communicate with the file server. The whole thing is controlled by a network operating system, such as Novell Netware.

dBASE IV is designed to run on PCs which are connected to a network in this way. The program itself runs on one or more of the

---

[1]There might, however, be difficulties with programs which rely on certain hardware characteristics of the PC (such as the loudspeaker or the 25-line screen) which might not be available on the terminal of the target machine.

PCs. The data files are stored on the file server and are therefore accessible to all users running dBASE IV on the LAN.

13.8.3 Client/server systems

A client/server system is an extension of the network concept described above. As well as the usual file server, the network also has a PC on which a **database server** program is run. A specific PC is usually reserved for this task, although this is not always the case.

A database server (also called a **back-end database**) is a special kind of database management system. One of its aims is to process SQL commands on behalf of other programs. These other programs are called **client programs** (or sometimes **front-end programs**), and they run on the other PCs on the network. Using SQL, the clients request an operation from the server. The server responds by 'serving' the resulting data back to the client.

One of the advantages of this approach is to reduce the amount of data that needs to be transported around the network, so speeding up the system considerably. This is because the client only has to send the SQL command to the server, and the server only returns the specific records which the client requested. This is in contrast to the file server approach, in which the SQL command is executed on the PC but the data is held on the file server. In order to select even a few records, the PC has to retrieve the entire table from the server. This results in much larger volumes of data being sent around the network (although the use of indexes can help reduce this volume).

A second advantage of a client/server system is that all control and security functions can be centralised at the server, where they are built into the data management system. This in turn simplifies the work of the front-end programs.

There is a special version of dBASE IV, called the dBASE IV Server Edition, which can be used as a front-end in a client/server network ('Server Edition' is a bit of a misnomer since dBASE IV does not itself act as the server; 'Client Edition' would be more apt).

The Server Edition has the advantage of being able to translate dBASE IV/SQL commands to the dialect of the server with which it is communicating (despite being a standard, SQL comes in many different dialects). Most dBASE IV/SQL applications which make use of embedded SQL – including all the examples in this book – could be transferred to a client/server system with little or no alteration.

13.8.4 Locking

In any database management system, problems would occur if two users were allowed to alter the same data at the same time. The usual way of avoiding this situation is with a system of **locks**. With this system, only one user can lock a given item of data at any one time. Once he or she has done so, others users are prevented from altering that data.

In dBASE IV's SQL mode, locking is automatic. Whenever a user attempts an operation which will alter an item of data, dBASE IV tries to lock the data. If it succeeds, it proceeds with the operation and then releases the lock. If it fails (because another user has already locked the data), it advises the user, then keeps on trying for a pre-defined period.

13.9 DBAs and data dictionaries

In most medium and large organisations which use centralised databases, there is a person (or group of people) known as the Database Administrator (DBA). The DBA is responsible for all the day-to-day management of the database.

One of the tools at the disposal of the DBA is a **data dictionary**. A data dictionary is itself a database. It contains information about all the data used within the organisation, including such details as field names and data types. The better data dictionaries go much further than this, and contain extensive information about how the data is to be processed and interpreted. They might, for example, include an indication of which application programs are allowed to access a specific table, or which departments can request a given report. This 'data about data' is sometimes called **meta-data**.

At one time, it was usual for the data dictionary to exist separately from the main database, requiring different commands and procedures to access it. A more modern approach – and clearly a more convenient one – is to integrate the data dictionary within the database. In this way, it can be consulted in exactly the same was as all the other data.

As far as dBASE IV/SQL is concerned, the data in the catalogue tables and in the SQLHOME database could be thought of as providing a data dictionary. However, it is a very rudimentary one because the meta-data is intended for the benefit of dBASE IV/SQL rather than the DBA.[1]

---

[1]C.J. Date suggests that the catalogue tables of the DB2 system (on which the structure of dBASE IV/SQL's catalogues are based) can be considered as a rudimentary data dictionary. He uses the term 'rudimentary' because they only contain information which the database management system itself needs (Date, 1990, p181).

13.10 Security

One of the responsibilities of the DBA is the security of the database.

The basis of any security system is the password. By issuing passwords to users, the DBA can control who can and cannot access the system. With a password system in force, all users must **log in** before being able to use the database. To do this, the users must first identify themselves to the computer by typing in their names. They then type the password. The computer checks the password against its internal list of authorised users, allowing access only if both items are correct.

In dBASE IV, the DBA uses a menu-driven system called PROTECT to define user names and passwords. One user name, SQLDBA, is permanently set up. This is the name that would normally be used by the DBA.

The SQLDBA can grant **privileges** to other uses. A privilege is a permission to access particular data in a particular way. In general, users cannot access anything unless they have been granted specific permission to do so. As an exception, all users have full privileges to the tables which they have themselves created. SQLDBA can also grant to other users the privilege of granting privileges.

SQLDBA has permission to do anything with the database, except for amending or deleting the catalogue tables.

SQL's GRANT command is used to give privileges to other users. For example, SQLDBA might use the following command to allow users Jackie and Pete to select existing rows from, and to add new rows to, the Property and Sales tables:

```
GRANT SELECT, INSERT
ON Property, Sales TO Jackie, Pete;
```

Similarly, the REVOKE command is used to withdraw privileges from users.

Privileges may be granted in respect of the following commands: SELECT, INSERT, DELETE, UPDATE, INDEX and ALTER. SQLDBA can grant privileges to any other user. A table can only be deleted by SQLDBA or the person who created it.

Even with a password system in force, a technically aware person could still gain access to the database, for example, by by-passing the dBASE IV security system entirely. To guard against this, dBASE IV has a facility for encrypting data. The effect of this is to make the data completely unintelligible, both within and outside the dBASE IV environment. The process can only be reversed by dBASE IV itself.

186

Only tables which were created after the security system was installed can be encrypted in this way.

13.11 Views

A view is a **virtual table**, that is, a combination of parts of one or more other tables. A view is a bit like a temporary table, but with two important differences. First, the view does not physically exist as a .DBF file on disk. Second, the view is **dynamic**. This means that, if the user alters the data in a view, the corresponding data in the underlying table is altered, and vice versa.

The following command creates a view, named LIMITED, which contains all the data from the Sales table except the names of buyers and sellers:

```
CREATE VIEW Limited
AS SELECT PropNum, SaleDate, Price
FROM Sales;
```

As far as the security system is concerned, a view behaves exactly like a table. Views can therefore be used in situations where it is desirable to grant users access to certain rows and columns but not to the entire table.

13.12 Transaction processing

It sometimes happens that, during a series of updates to a database, a problem occurs that prevents the updates from finishing normally. For example, if one user leaves an item of data locked for a long time, this would prevent other programs from altering that data. In some applications, when a series of related updates is interrupted in this way, the data could become corrupted or its integrity could be lost.

To help guard against this situation, dBASE IV/SQL has a facility for creating a **log file**. This is a file which records the results of critical updates. Then, if a problem occurs, the information in the file can be used to 'undo' the updates, that is, to return the database to the state it was in before the updates started.

dBASE IV's BEGIN TRANSACTION command is used to open the log file. If the updates finish normally, the END TRANSACTION command is issued to close the log file. If a problem occurs which prevents the updates from finishing normally, the ROLLBACK command can be used to 'roll back' the database to the state it was in immediately before BEGIN TRANSACTION was issued.

CHAPTER FOURTEEN

Useful commands and functions

See Section 6.12 for an explanation of the syntax used in this chapter.

14.1 SQL commands

ALTER TABLE

SQL command

Purpose:	Adds new columns to an existing table.
Syntax:	ALTER TABLE <table name>
	ADD <column name> <data type>
	[<column name> <data type> ...];
Example:	ALTER TABLE Property
	ADD (PropType CHAR(20), Size
	SMALLINT);
Described in:	7.5

CLOSE

Embedded SQL command

Purpose:	Closes an SQL cursor.
Syntax:	CLOSE <cursor name>;
Example:	CLOSE MyCursor;
Described in:	11.4
See also:	DECLARE CURSOR, OPEN, FETCH INTO

CREATE DATABASE

SQL command

Purpose:	Creates an empty SQL database.
Syntax:	CREATE DATABASE [<path>]
	<database name>
Example:	CREATE DATABASE Housing

Described in:	3.3, 3.4
See also:	CREATE TABLE, DROP DATABASE

CREATE INDEX

SQL command

Purpose:	Creates an index from one or more columns of a table in order to speed up searching.
Syntax:	CREATE [UNIQUE] INDEX \<index name\>
	ON \<table name\>
	(\<column name\> [ASC/DESC]
	[, \<column name\> [ASC/DESC] ...);
Examples:	CREATE INDEX SalesNdx
	ON Sales (PropNum);
	CREATE UNIQUE INDEX Sold
	ON Sales (PropNum);
	CREATE INDEX SellrInd
	ON Sales (PropNum, Buyer, Seller);
Described in:	7.6, 7.6.1

CREATE TABLE

SQL command

Purpose:	Creates one or more new SQL table.
Syntax:	CREATE TABLE \<table name\>;
	(\<column name\> \<data type\>
	[,\<column name\> \<data type\> ...]);
Example:	CREATE TABLE Property
	(PropNum INTEGER, HouseNum CHAR(6),
	YearC SMALLINT, Conditn CHAR(1));
Described in:	4.3

DBDEFINE

SQL command

Purpose:	Stores a description of one or more dBASE data files in the catalogue tables.
Syntax:	DBDEFINE [\<DBF filename\>];
Example:	DBDEFINE;
	(When no DBF filename is specified, the command creates entries for all DBF files in the directory of the current SQL database which do not already have catalogue entries.)
Described in:	6.11, 8.4

189

DECLARE CURSOR

Embedded SQL command

Purpose:	Defines a cursor.
Syntax:	DECLARE <cursor name> CURSOR
	FOR <SELECT command>
	[FOR UPDATE OF <column name>,
	<column name> ...]
Example:	DECLARE MyCursor CURSOR
	FOR SELECT HouseNum, Street, YearC
	FROM Property
	WHERE HouseNum=VHouse
	AND Street LIKE VStreet
	FOR UPDATE OF HouseNum, Street,
	YearC;
Described in:	11.4
See also:	OPEN, CLOSE, FETCH INTO, UPDATE/
	WHERE CURRENT OF, DELETE FROM/WHERE
	CURRENT OF

DELETE

SQL command

Purpose:	Deletes rows from a table.
Syntax:	DELETE FROM <table name>
	[WHERE clause];
Example:	DELETE FROM Property
	WHERE Street = 'Wellington St.';
Described in:	7.2
See also:	DELETE FROM/WHERE CURRENT OF

DELETE FROM/WHERE CURRENT OF

Embedded SQL command

Purpose:	Deletes rows referenced by the cursor.
Syntax:	DELETE FROM <table name>
	WHERE CURRENT OF <cursor name>;
Example:	DELETE FROM Property
	WHERE CURRENT OF MyCursor;
Described in:	11.4
See also:	DECLARE CURSOR, OPEN, CLOSE, FETCH
	INTO, UPDATE/WHERE CURRENT OF

DROP DATABASE

SQL command

Purpose:	Deletes an SQL database.
Syntax:	`DROP DATABASE <database name>;`
Example:	`DROP DATABASE Housing;`
Described in:	7.4
See also:	`DROP TABLE`

DROP TABLE

SQL command

Purpose:	Deletes an SQL table.
Syntax:	`DROP TABLE <table name>;`
Example:	`DROP TABLE Sales;`
Described in:	7.3
See also:	`DROP DATABASE`

FETCH INTO

Embedded SQL command

Purpose:	Advances the cursor by one row and copies the values from the selected row to dBASE variables.
Syntax:	`FETCH <cursor name>` `INTO <variable>, <variable> ... ;`
Example:	`FETCH MyCursor` `INTO VHouse, VStreet, VYear`
Described in:	11.4
See also:	`DECLARE CURSOR, OPEN, CLOSE, DELETE FROM/WHERE CURRENT OF, UPDATE/WHERE CURRENT OF`

INSERT

SQL command

Purpose:	Adds a new row to a table.
Syntax:	`INSERT INTO <table name>` `VALUES <list of values>;`

Example:	`INSERT INTO Property`
	`VALUES (1,'Wellington St.','1212',`
	`1899,'P');`

Described in:	4.4
See also:	`LOAD DATA`

191

LOAD DATA

SQL command

Purpose:	Loads data from a file into an SQL table.

Syntax:	`LOAD DATA FROM <file name>`
	`INTO TABLE <table name>`
	`[TYPE DELIMITED/SDF];`

Example:	`LOAD DATA FROM InProp.Txt` `INTO TABLE Property TYPE DELIMITED;`
Described in:	13.4
See also:	`INSERT`

OPEN

Embedded SQL command

Purpose:	Opens a cursor and positions the pointer before the first row of the result table.
Syntax:	`OPEN <cursor name>;`
Example:	`OPEN MyCursor;`
Described in:	11.4
See also:	`DECLARE CURSOR, CLOSE`

SELECT

SQL command

Purpose:	Retrieves data from one or more tables.

Syntax:	`<SELECT clause>`
	`[<INTO clause>]`
	`<FROM clause>`
	`[<WHERE clause>]`
	`[<GROUP BY clause>`
	`[<HAVING clause>]]`
	`[UNION <subquery>] ...`
	`[<ORDER BY clause> /`
	`<FOR UPDATE OF clause>]`
	`[<SAVE TO TEMP clause>];`

Example:	`SELECT Buyer, AVG(Price)`
	`FROM Sales`
	`WHERE Buyer LIKE '*Ltd*'`
	`GROUP BY Buyer`
	`HAVING AVG(Price) > 25000;`

Described in:	Chapters 5 and 6

SHOW DATABASE

    SQL command

    Purpose: Shows which databases are available in the system.

    Syntax: `SHOW DATABASE;`

    Described in: 3.2

START DATABASE

    SQL command

    Purpose: Opens an SQL database.

    Syntax: `START DATABASE <database name>`

    Example: `START DATABASE Housing;`

    Described in: 3.2

STOP DATABASE

    SQL command

    Purpose: Closes the current database.

    Syntax: `STOP DATABASE;`

    Described in: 3.7

UNLOAD DATA

    SQL command

    Purpose: Creates a data file (such as a DBF file) and copies data to it from an SQL table.

    Syntax:
```
UNLOAD DATA TO [path]
<data file name>
FROM TABLE <table name>
[TYPE DELIMITED];
```

    Example: `UNLOAD DATA TO Temp.Dbf FROM Sales;`

    Described in: 13.5

    See also: `LOAD DATA`

UPDATE

    SQL command

    Purpose: Alters the data in the selected rows of the table.

    Syntax:
```
UPDATE <table name>
SET <column name> = <value>
[,<column name> = <value> ... ]
[WHERE <search condition>];
```

    Example:
```
UPDATE Property
SET Conditn = 'G'
```

WHERE Street = 'Wellington St.';

Described in: 7.1

See also: UPDATE/WHERE CURRENT OF

UPDATE/WHERE CURRENT OF
Embedded SQL command

Purpose: Alters the data in the rows pointed to by the cursor.

Syntax: UPDATE <table name>
SET <column name> = <value>
[,<column name> = <value> ...]
WHERE CURRENT OF <cursor name>;

Example: UPDATE Property
SET HouseNum = VNum,
Street = VStreet, YearC = VYear,
Conditn = VConditn
WHERE CURRENT OF MyCursor;

Described in: 11.4

See also: DECLARE CURSOR, OPEN, CLOSE, FETCH INTO, DELETE FROM/WHERE CURRENT OF

14.2 SQL functions

AVG
SQL function

Purpose: Calculates the mean average of a numeric column over a range of selected rows.

Syntax: AVG([ALL/DISTINCT] <column name>)

or: AVG([ALL] <expression based on columns>)

Example: SELECT AVG(Price) FROM Sales
WHERE Buyer = 'Vista Estates Ltd';

SELECT AVG(Y.Price - X.Price),
X.Buyer FROM Sales X, Sales Y
WHERE X.PropNum = Y.PropNum
AND X.Buyer = Y.Seller;
(This example calculates the average profit achieved as a result of the purchase and subsequent resale of a property.)

Described in: 5.9

COUNT

SQL function

Purpose:	Counts the number of selected rows.
Syntax:	COUNT(*/[DISTINCT]<column name>)
Example:	SELECT COUNT(*) FROM Sales WHERE Price > 25000; SELECT COUNT(DISTINCT Buyer) FROM Sales;
Described in:	5.9

MAX

SQL function

Purpose:	Determines the highest value from a numeric column over a range of selected rows.
Syntax:	MAX([ALL/DISTINCT] <column name>)
or:	MAX([ALL] <expression based on columns>)
Example:	SELECT MAX(Price) FROM Sales WHERE Buyer = 'Vista Estates Ltd'; SELECT MAX(Y.Price - X.Price), X.Buyer FROM Sales X, Sales Y WHERE X.PropNum = Y.PropNum AND X.Buyer = Y.Seller; (This example calculates the maximum profit achieved as a result of the purchase and subsequent resale of a property.)
Described in:	5.9

MIN

SQL function

Purpose:	Determines the lowest value from a numeric column over a range of selected rows.
Syntax:	MIN([ALL/DISTINCT] <column name>)
or:	MIN([ALL] <expression based on columns>)
Example:	SELECT MIN(Price) FROM Sales WHERE Buyer = 'Vista Estates Ltd'; SELECT MIN(Y.Price - X.Price), X.Buyer FROM Sales X, Sales Y

```
WHERE X.PropNum = Y.PropNum
AND X.Buyer = Y.Seller;
```
(This example calculates the minimum profit achieved as a result of the purchase and subsequent resale of a property.)

Described in: 5.9

SUM

SQL function

Purpose: Calculates the total of a numeric column over a range of selected rows.

Syntax: `SUM([ALL/DISTINCT] <column name>)`

or: `SUM([ALL] <expression based on columns>)`

Example:
```
SELECT SUM(Price) FROM Sales
WHERE Buyer = 'Vista Estates Ltd';

SELECT SUM(Y.Price - X.Price),
X.Buyer FROM Sales X, Sales Y
WHERE X.PropNum = Y.PropNum
AND X.Buyer = Y.Seller;
```
(This example calculates the total profit achieved as a result of the purchase and subsequent resale of a property.)

Described in: 5.9

14.3 dBASE commands

?

dBASE command used in programs

Purpose: Writes the result of an expression on the screen after first moving the cursor to a new row.

Syntax: `? <expression>`

Example: `? 4 * 5`

Described in: 10.4

See also: ??

??

dBASE command used in programs

Purpose: Like ? but does not move the cursor to a new row.

Described in:	10.5.1
See also:	?

@/SAY/GET

dBASE command used in programs

Purpose:	Specifies input and output in an on-screen form.
Syntax:	@ <row>,<column> SAY <expression> [GET <variable>] [PICTURE]
Example:	@ 5,3 SAY 'Street' GET VStreet
	@ 7,3 SAY 'Condition' GET VConditn PICTURE '####' (The PICTURE clause specifies that the input field may contain up to four characters.)
Described in:	10.8

ACCEPT

dBASE command used in programs

Purpose:	Used in programs to accept input from the user. ACCEPT creates a character variable and displays a prompt on the screen. The user can then type some text. When the user presses the Enter key, the text is stored in the variable.
Syntax:	ACCEPT [<prompt>] TO <variable>
Example:	ACCEPT 'What is your name' TO VName
Described in:	10.5
See also:	WAIT

ACTIVATE POPUP

dBASE command used in programs

Purpose:	Activates a pop-up menu (which must already have been defined).
Syntax:	ACTIVATE POPUP <popup menu name>
Described in:	13.3
See also:	DEFINE POPUP, DEACTIVATE POPUP, BAR (dBASE function)

APPEND

Full-screen dBASE command; can be used in SQL mode

Purpose:	Allows the user to add records to a table by filling in a form.

Syntax:	APPEND
Described in:	8.3
See also:	BROWSE, EDIT

BROWSE

Full-screen dBASE command; can be used in SQL mode

Purpose:	Allows the user to page through a table, and to alter and add records.
Syntax:	BROWSE
Described in:	8.3
See also:	EDIT, APPEND

CLEAR

dBASE command used in programs

Purpose:	Clears the screen and places the cursor in the top-left corner.
Syntax:	CLEAR
Described in:	10.8

CLOSE ALTERNATE

dBASE command

Purpose:	Closes the 'alternate' file (that is, the file in which screen output is being saved).
Syntax:	CLOSE ALTERNATE
Described in:	3.6
See also:	SET ALTERNATE ON/OFF, SET ALTERNATE TO

CLOSE DATABASES

dBASE command; cannot be used in SQL mode

Purpose:	Closes all open dBASE data files (that is, DBF files which were opened with USE).
Syntax:	CLOSE DATABASES
Described in:	8.4
See also:	USE

CREATE

Full-screen dBASE command; can be used in SQL mode

Purpose:	Creates a dBASE data file (DBF file).
Syntax:	CREATE <filename>
Example:	CREATE Shops
Described in:	8.4
See also:	USE, CLOSE DATABASE

DEACTIVATE POPUP

dBASE command used in programs

Purpose:	Removes a pop-up menu from the screen. Control returns to the point at which the pop-up was activated.
Syntax:	DEACTIVATE POPUP
Described in:	13.3
See also:	DEFINE POPUP, ACTIVATE POPUP, BAR (dBASE function)

DEBUG

dBASE command for interactive use

Purpose:	Invokes dBASE IV's built-in debugger
Syntax:	DEBUG <program name>
Example:	DEBUG Interest.Prs
Described in:	10.15

DEFINE POPUP

dBASE command used in programs

Purpose:	Defines a pop-up menu.
Syntax:	DEFINE POPUP <popup name> FROM <row>,<column>

```
DEFINE BAR <number> OF <popup name>
PROMPT <text>
    .
    .
    .

ON SELECTION POPUP <popup name>
DO <procedure name>
```

Described in:	13.3
See also:	ACTIVATE POPUP, DEACTIVATE POPUP, BAR (dBASE function)

DO <name>

dBASE command

Purpose:	Runs a program or a procedure.
Syntax:	DO <program name>/<procedure name>
Example:	DO Info
Described in:	10.3, 11.6

DO CASE/ENDCASE

dBASE command used in programs

Purpose: Chooses one possibility from a series of alternatives.

Syntax:

```
DO CASE
  CASE <condition>
    <commands>
  CASE <condition>
    <commands>

       .
       .
       .

  OTHERWISE
    <commands>
ENDCASE
```

Example:

```
ACCEPT 'Which day is it? ' TO TODAY
DO CASE
  CASE TODAY = 'saturday'
    ? 'It is the weekend'
  CASE TODAY = 'monday'
    ? 'Monday morning!'
  CASE TODAY = 'tuedsay'
    ? 'The week is still young'
  CASE TODAY = 'thursday'
    ? 'Soon be the weekend again'
ENDCASE
```

Described in: 10.13
See also: IF/ELSE/ENDIF

DO WHILE/ENDDO

dBASE command used in programs

Purpose: Executes a series of commands repeatedly for as long as a given condition is true.

Syntax:

```
DO WHILE <condition>
  <commands>
ENDDO
```

Example:

```
STORE 0 TO COUNTER
DO WHILE COUNTER < 10
  ? 'Greetings'
  STORE COUNTER + 1 TO COUNTER
ENDDO
```

Described in: 10.14

EDIT

Full-screen dBASE command; can be used in SQL mode

Purpose:	Displays records and allows the user to alter them.
Syntax:	EDIT
Described in:	8.3
See also:	BROWSE

ERASE

dBASE command; can also be used in SQL mode

Purpose:	Deletes a data file.
Syntax:	ERASE \<data file name>/?
	The file extension must always be specified.
	ERASE ? displays a list of files from which a selection can be made.
Example:	ERASE TEMP.DBF
Described in:	7.5

HELP

dBASE command for interactive use

Purpose:	Invokes dBASE IV's interactive help system.
Syntax:	HELP

IF/ELSE/ENDIF

dBASE command used in programs

Purpose:	Executes one or other series of instructions according to the value of a condition.
Syntax:	IF \<condition>
	\<commands>
	[ELSE
	\<commands>]
	ENDIF

Example:	? 'Do you want the sum or average?'
	ACCEPT 'Enter s or a' TO Choice
	?
	IF CHOICE = 's'
	? 'Sum is: ' + STR(Q1+Q2)
	ELSE
	? 'Average is: ' + STR((Q1+Q2)/2)
	ENDIF
Described in:	10.12
See also:	DO CASE

MODIFY FILE

> dBASE command for interactive use
> Purpose: Invokes dBASE IV's built-in text editor.
> Syntax: `MODIFY FILE <file name>`
> Example: `MODIFY FILE Profits.Prs`
> Described in: 10.2, Appendix A

PROCEDURE

> dBASE command used in programs
> Purpose: Indicates the start of a procedure (a
>   subroutine).
> Syntax: `PROCEDURE <procedure name>`
> Example: `PROCEDURE TownName`
>   `? 'London'`
>   `RETURN`
> Described in: 11.6
> See also: `RETURN`

QUIT

> dBASE command
> Purpose: Closes all open files and exits dBASE IV.
> Syntax: `QUIT`
> Described in: 3.7

READ

> dBASE command used in programs
> Purpose: Passes control to an on-screen form. The
>   values which the user types into the fields
>   (specified by GETs) are stored in the
>   corresponding variables.
> Syntax: `READ`
> Example: `@ 5,3 SAY 'Forename? ' GET FName`
>   `@ 6,3 SAY 'Surname?  ' GET LName`
>   `READ`
> Described in: 10.8
> See also: `@/SAY/GET`

RETURN

> dBASE command used in programs
> Purpose: In procedures, returns control to the
>   command following the command which

invoked the procedure. In the main program, returns control to dBASE.

Syntax:	RETURN
Described in:	11.6
See also:	PROCEDURE

SET ALTERNATE ON/OFF

dBASE command

Purpose:	Controls the saving of screen output in a text file (which must already have been opened by SET ALTERNATE TO).
Described in:	3.6
See also:	SET ALTERNATE TO

SET ALTERNATE TO

dBASE command

Purpose:	Opens a text file for saving screen output.
Syntax:	SET ALTERNATE TO <file name>
Described in:	3.6
See also:	SET ALTERNATE ON/OFF

SET EXACT ON/OFF

dBASE command

Purpose:	When On, character strings must be equal in both length and value for an equality test to succeed (default: Off).
Described in:	10.10

SET PAUSE ON/OFF

dBASE command

Purpose:	When On, output from a SELECT command pauses when the screen in full until the user presses a key (default: Off).
Described in:	12.7

SET SQL ON/OFF

dBASE command; cannot be used in programs

Purpose:	Switches between dBASE and SQL modes.
Described in:	3.1

SET STATUS ON/OFF

dBASE command

Purpose:	Hides or displays the dBASE IV status bar.

SET TALK ON/OFF

dBASE command, mainly used in programs

Purpose:	Switches certain dBASE messages on and off.

STORE

dBASE command used in programs

Purpose:	Assigns a value to a variable, creating the variable if necessary.
Syntax:	`STORE <expression> TO <variable>`
Example:	`STORE 7 * 3 TO QUANT`
Described in:	10.7

TYPE

dBASE command

Purpose:	Displays or prints the contents of a text file.
Syntax:	`TYPE <file name> [TO PRINTER]`
Example:	`TYPE MyWork.Txt TO PRINTER`
Described in:	3.6

USE

dBASE command; can be used in SQL mode

Purpose:	Opens a dBASE data file (that is, a DBF file).
Syntax:	`USE <data file name>`
Example:	`USE Shops`
Described in:	8.2
See also:	`CLOSE DATABASES`

WAIT

dBASE command used in programs

Purpose:	Halts a program until the user presses a key. The character which the user types can optionally be stored in a variable.
Syntax:	`WAIT [prompt] [TO variable]`
Example:	`WAIT 'Your choice?' TO CHOICE`
Described in:	11.3.1
See also:	`ACCEPT`

14.4 dBASE functions

BAR

dBASE function

Purpose:	Returns the number of the option most recently selected from a popup menu.
Syntax:	`BAR( )`
Described in:	13.3
See also:	`DEFINE POPUP, ACTIVATE POPUP, DEACTIVATE POPUP`

LEN

dBASE function

Purpose:	Returns the length of a character expression.
Syntax:	`LEN(<expression>)`
Described in:	10.11.2

LOWER

dBASE function

Purpose:	Converts a character string to lower case.
Syntax:	`LOWER(<expression>)`
Example:	`? LOWER('Ballerton D.C.')`
	Result: `ballerton d.c.`
Described in:	10.11

LTRIM

dBASE function

Purpose:	Removes leading spaces from a character string.
Syntax:	`LTRIM(<expression>)`
Example:	`STORE 'Cat' TO LeftStr`
	`STORE '      astrophe' TO RightStr`
	`? LeftStr+LTRIM(RightStr)`
	Result: `Catastrophe`
Described in:	10.11
See also:	`TRIM`

TRIM

dBASE function

Purpose: Removes trailing spaces from a character string.

Syntax: `TRIM(<expression>)`

Example:
```
STORE 'Casa        ' TO LeftStr
STORE 'Blanca      ' TO RightStr
? TRIM(LeftStr)+SPACE(1)+RightStr
Result: Casa Blanca
```

Described in: 10.11

See also: `LTRIM`

RAND

dBASE function

Purpose: Generates a random number between zero and one.

Syntax: `RAND()`

Example: `STORE RAND() TO Quant`

Described in: 10.14

ROUND

dBASE function

Purpose: Rounds a numeric expression to a specified number of decimal places.

Syntax: `ROUND(<expression>,<no. of places>)`

Example:
```
STORE 0.5512 TO Qty
? ROUND(QTY,2)
Result: 0.55
```

Described in: 10.14

SPACE

dBASE function

Purpose: Returns a string of spaces.

Syntax: `SPACE(<no. of spaces>)`

Example: `STORE SPACE(20) TO VStreet`

Described in: 10.11

STR

dBASE function

Purpose: Converts a numeric expression to a character string.

206

Syntax:	STR(<expression>[,<length>[,<no. of decimal places]])
Example:	STORE 2.754 TO Qty
	? STR(Qty,5,2)
	Result: 2.75
Described in:	10.11.3
See also:	VAL

VAL

dBASE function

Purpose:	Converts a character string to a number.
Syntax:	VAL(<expression>)
Example:	ACCEPT 'Exchange rate? ' TO Rate
	STORE VAL(Rate) TO Rate
	? 'You will receive',
	Rate * Amount, 'Dollars'
Described in:	10.11.3

Using the built-in text editor

A.1 Loading the editor

To invoke the built-in text editor, issue a command in the form:

```
MODI FILE filename
```

For example:

```
MODI FILE Doctors.Prs
```

A.2 Moving the cursor

Once inside the editor, press the arrow keys to move the cursor up, down, left and right. To scroll through the file one screen at a time, press PgUp and PgDn. The Home key moves the cursor to the start of the line; the End key moves it to the end of the line.

A.3 Saving your work

To save the file and exit the editor, press Ctrl-End. If you want to close the editor without saving your work, press Esc.

A.4 Deleting text

Use the Del key to delete the character at the current cursor position, or Backspace to delete the character to the left of the cursor. Ctrl-Y deletes the line containing the cursor.

To delete a larger block of text, proceed as follows:

(a)   Move the cursor to the start of the block.
(b)   Press f6.

(c)   Move the cursor to the end of block (you will see the block highlighted as you move the cursor).

(d)   When you have finished marking the block in this way, press Enter.

(e)   Press the Del key to delete the block.

A.5 Moving a block of text

To move a block of text to another part of the file:

(a)   Move the cursor to the start of the block.

(b)   Press f6.

(c)   Move the cursor to the end of block (you will see the block highlighted as you move the cursor).

(d)   When you have finished marking the block in this way, press Enter.

(e)   Move the cursor to the point to which you wish to move the block.

(f)   Press f7.

A.6 Copying a block of text

To create a copy of a block of text and place it elsewhere in the file:

(a)   Move the cursor to the start of the block.

(b)   Press f6.

(c)   Move the cursor to the end of block (you will see the block highlighted as you move the cursor).

(d)   When you have finished marking the block in this way, press Enter.

(e)   Move the cursor to the point at which you wish the copy to appear.

(f)   Press f8.

A.7 Reading in another file

It is often useful to be able to merge several separate programs into a larger one. This can be achieved as follows:

(a)   In the current file, move the cursor to the point at which you wish to bring in another file.

(b)   Press f10 to invoke the editor's menu.

(c)   Select the 'Words' option, then the 'Read/write text file' sub-option, then 'Read text file'.

(d)   dBASE IV will prompt you for the name of the file which you wish to read in.

After you have specified the required file name, dBASE IV will copy the text from that file into the main file.

A.8 Further options

By pressing f10 from within the editor, you gain access to the editor's menu. Menu options are available for searching for a specified character string and for jumping to a given line number. You can also print the file, or write a marked block of text to a new file.

If the dBASE IV status bar is visible (it is switched on by issuing SET STATUS ON before invoking the editor, or by placing STATUS=ON in the Config.Db file), it will show the number of the line currently holding the cursor.

The sample database

To create the sample Housing database used in this book, proceed as follows.

First create a text file called NewProps.Txt. Use any text editor for this, such as the one built into dBASE IV (see Appendix A). The file should contain the following lines:

```
1,121,Wellington St.,1899,A
2,123,Wellington St.,1899,A
3,119,Wellington St.,1899,A
4,117,Wellington St.,1899,A
5,115,Wellington St.,1899,P
6,113,Wellington St.,1898,P
7,111,Wellington St.,1898,P
8,109,Wellington St.,1898,P
9,120,Park Road,1898,P
10,122,Park Road,1898,G
```

Then create a second text file, called NewSales.Txt, with the following contents:

```
1,19800225,25000,FX Properties Ltd,P Johnson
6,19811201,22500,Vista Estates Ltd,T Taylor
1,19800226,40000,Vista Estates Ltd,FX Properties Ltd
1,19800227,50000,Ballerton D.C.,Vista Estates Ltd
3,19811111,17500,Ballerton D.C.,T Zander
8,19820101,20000,Vista Estates Ltd,L Lauder
9,19820130,30000,Vista Estates Ltd,W Bendix
10,19830505,35000,FX Properties Ltd,I Stevenson
10,19830522,37500,Vista Estates Ltd,FX Properties Ltd
```

Finally, issue these commands, in SQL mode:

```
CREATE DATABASE Housing;
CREATE TABLE Property
(PropNum INTEGER, HouseNum CHAR(6), Street CHAR(20),
YearC SMALLINT, Conditn CHAR(1));
CREATE TABLE Sales
(PropNum INTEGER, SaleDate DATE, Price INTEGER,
Buyer CHAR(20), Seller CHAR(20));
LOAD DATA FROM NewProps.Txt
INTO TABLE Property TYPE DELIMITED;
LOAD DATA FROM NewSales.Txt
INTO TABLE Sales TYPE DELIMITED;
CREATE TABLE HelpTab
(H_Type CHAR(8), H_Number INTEGER);
INSERT INTO HelpTab
VALUES ('Previous', 0);
```

Exercises

C.1 Searches using the Housing database

These exercises relate to the material on single-table searches in Chapter 5. The information in Chapters 2 and 3 is also relevant, as is the material on data types in Section 4.2. Appendix B describes how the Housing database may be created.

C.1.1   Name each of the streets in the database.

C.1.2   List the properties in order of year of construction, the oldest first.

C.1.3   List the properties in order of year of construction, the newest first.

C.1.4   List the properties in Park Road.

C.1.5   List the properties in Wellington Street, sorted by year of construction.

C.1.6   List the properties in Wellington Street, just showing the year of construction and the condition.

C.1.7   List the properties which were built before 1899.

C.1.8   Which properties in the database are not in Wellington Street?

C.1.9   Give the property number of all properties sold before 1982.

C.1.10 Which properties in Wellington Street were built before 1899?

C.1.11 Which properties were built before 1899 and are not in Wellington Street?

C.1.12 Which properties are in average or poor condition?

C.1.13 Give the property numbers of the properties which were bought by a company whose name begins with 'Vista'.

C.1.14 Which sellers have an 'a' in the fourth character position of their names?

C.1.15   List the selling price for each sale, in dollars (assume that two dollars equals one pound).

C.1.16   List the property numbers of the properties which were sold for between £20,000 and £25,000.

C.1.17   How many different streets are there?

C.1.18   Produce a list showing the average price paid by each buyer.

The following exercises are based on the material on multiple-table searches given in Chapter 6.

C.1.19   Give the addresses of all properties sold before 1982.

C.1.20   Give the addresses of all properties sold for more than £30,000.

C.1.21   Give the addresses of all properties sold for between £20,000 and £25,000.

C.1.22   What are the addresses of the properties which were bought by Vista Estates? (Do this with a join.)

C.1.23   What are the addresses of the properties which were bought by Vista Estates? (Do this with a sub-select.)

C.1.24   Give all the information known about 121 Wellington Street, including details of its sales.

C.1.25   Produce a list of the limited companies which are active in the housing market, with an indication of the maximum price that each one has paid. (Tip: refer to Section 5.10.)

C.1.26   How many properties were bought and subsequently resold? (Tip: refer to Section 6.3.1.)

C.1.27   Give, for each buyer, the property number and price of the cheapest property which that buyer has purchased. (Tip: refer to Section 6.9).

C.2 Creating databases and tables

C.2.1   Create a database of the clubs and societies in a town. Use the following tables:

```
Table: People
Person          Age     Occupation
Jackson         66      Manager
Peters          55      Author
Vickers         33      Manager
Younghusband    44      Clerk
```

```
Table: Clubs
Person              Club
Jackson             Opera
Jackson             Rambling
Jackson             Brass band
Peters              Rambling
Peters              Brass band
Vickers             Opera
Younghusband        Rambling
```

C.2.2   List the societies which exist in the town.
C.2.3   How many managers are there?
C.2.4   Sort the residents by occupation.
C.2.5   Which residents have a 'd' in their name?
C.2.6   List the societies which have managers as members.
C.2.7   Of which societies are all members over 50?

C.3 Database design

The computer is not used in this exercise.

A study into joint ventures has produced a mass of data concerning multinational companies, including their turnover figures, profits and numbers of employees. We wish to use a database to answer questions along the lines of: 'Are there more joint ventures between Japanese and European companies than between Japanese and US ones?'. (Assume that information about the nationalities of the companies is also available.)

Design a database that can make use of the data from the study to answer these sorts of questions. Show your design in the form of a block diagram.

C.4 Elementary programming

The exercises in this section can also be carried out with dBASE III Plus.

C.4.1 Write a program which does the following:

(a)   Prompts the user for his surname.
(b)   Prompts the user for his first name.
(c)   Displays a personalised greeting on the screen, incorporating the names which the user typed in.

C.4.2 Write a program which accepts an amount of money in

French francs and displays the corresponding amount in pounds, assuming a rate of nine francs to the pound. Use a form for the input.

C.4.3 Modify the program in C.4.2 so that, after the result has been displayed, the program gives the user the option of repeating the calculation with another value. (Use a DO WHILE loop for this.)

C.5 Embedded SQL

Write a query program for the Sales table. The program should ask the user to type in a name of a buyer, then display all the transactions for that buyer.

C.6 Creating an application

Suppose that you are conducting a study into the relationships which exist between the worlds of politics and property. You decide to set up a database containing information about politicians and any dealings which they may have in the property sector.

Design a database to hold the following data: the name of the politician; his or her party; his or her main political function; and details of any side-lines which the politician has in the property world. Write an application for maintaining this database.

This could be a very time-consuming exercise. However, you can save time by adopting the following strategy. Create two tables for the database: one with the names, parties and main political functions of the politicians; the other with details of the side-lines. There will be a one-to-many relationship between these two tables. You can therefore use the sample Housing.Prs (in Chapter 12) and Housing1.Prs (in Section 13.3) programs as a framework for your application.

Common problems

This appendix gives answers to some of the problems most frequently faced by newcomers to SQL.

Problem: dBASE IV/SQL displays the message 'No database open'.
Solution: You cannot perform any operation on a database until you have first opened it. You do this with a command such as:

```
START DATABASE Housing;
```

Problem: dBASE IV/SQL displays 'Incomplete SQL statement' when I type the following:

```
SELECT *
FROM Property
```

Solution: You forgot the semi-colon at the end of the command.

Problem: When I typed the following command, no results were displayed, just the SQL prompt:

```
SELECT *
FROM Property
WHERE Street = 'WELLINGTON ST.';
```

Solution: Although the query was syntactically correct, the result table was empty. This was because the relevant street in the table is Wellington St., but you searched for WELLINGTON ST. In this context, dBASE IV/SQL is sensitive to the difference between capitals and lower case.

Problem: dBASE IV/SQL issued the message 'Variable not found' when I typed:

```
SELECT Property
FROM Property
WHERE Street = 'Wellington St.';
```

Solution: The names which appear after the word SELECT must be those of the columns which you want to appear in the result table. In this case, there is no column called Property.

Problem: dBASE IV/SQL said 'Variable not found' when I typed the following:

```
SELECT PropNum
FROM Property
WHERE SaleDate < {01/01/1982}
AND HouseNum = '121'
AND Street = 'Wellington St.';
```

Solution: The names which immediately follow the word FROM indicate the tables which are to be searched – in this case, just the Property table. But SaleDate is a column in the Sales table. SQL only looks at the tables which are explicitly listed in the FROM clause, so SaleDate is, at this point, unknown to SQL. It therefore issues the 'Variable not found' message.

Problem: How can I find out which columns and tables exist in the database?
Solution: By examining the special catalogue tables. Use the following command:

```
SELECT colname, coltype, collen, tbname
FROM syscols
WHERE NOT tbname LIKE 'SYS%';
```

Problem: Do the columns in the WHERE clause also have to be specified in the SELECT clause?
Solution: No, this is not essential. The columns listed immediately after the word SELECT are those which are to appear in the result table.

Problem: When I typed the following command, dBASE IV/SQL responded with the message 'Group by columns must be specified in SELECT clause':

```
SELECT AVG(Price)
FROM Sales
GROUP BY Buyer;
```

Solution: This query is asking for the average price per buyer but the Buyer column has not been specified in the SELECT clause. SQL cannot perform a grouping on the basis of a column which does not appear in the result table.

Problem: I received the message 'All select items must be group by columns or aggregate functions' when I typed:

```
SELECT PropNum, Buyer, AVG(Price)
FROM Sales
GROUP BY Buyer;
```

Solution: The following command would have been correct:

```
SELECT Buyer, AVG(Price)
FROM Sales
GROUP BY Buyer;
```

This asks for the average price per buyer. In the incorrect version shown above, the PropNum was also specified in the SELECT clause. But what PropNum is this? There is no such thing as a property number for a given average price, so the query does not make sense. Whenever a SELECT command contains a GROUP BY clause, the items immediately following the word SELECT must be either aggregate functions or the same columns that are used in the GROUP BY clause.

Problem: With the following command, I got the message 'Keyword FROM expected':

```
SELECT HouseNum, Street,
FROM Property;
```

Solution: The fault lies in the extra comma which has crept in after the word Street.

Problem: The following produced far more output than I was expecting:

219

```
SELECT HouseNum, Street
FROM Property, Sales
WHERE Buyer = 'Vista Estates Ltd.';
```

Solution: By omitting the join condition:

```
WHERE Property.PropNum = Sales.PropNum
```

you have asked for every possible combination of rows from the two tables.

Problem: dBASE IV/SQL displayed the message 'Ambiguous column name PROPNUM' when I typed:

```
SELECT PropNum, HouseNum, Street, Price
FROM Property, Sales
WHERE Property.PropNum = Sales.PropNum;
```

Solution: Where the same column name occurs in more than one table, you must prefix it with the table name. Either of the following would have been correct:

```
SELECT Property.PropNum, HouseNum, Street, Price
FROM Property, Sales
WHERE Property.PropNum = Sales.PropNum;
```

or:

```
SELECT Sales.PropNum, HouseNum, Street, Price
FROM Property, Sales
WHERE Property.PropNum = Sales.PropNum;
```

Problem: dBASE IV/SQL reported 'Keyword FROM expected'. The command was:

```
SELECT HouseNum, Street
FROM Property
WHERE PropNum IN
  (SELECT PropNum, Buyer
  FROM Sales
  WHERE Buyer LIKE 'Vista*'
   AND Property.PropNum = Sales.PropNum);
```

Solution: The outer SELECT expects the inner SELECT to produce a table of property numbers. In fact, the inner SELECT produces a table of property numbers and buyers. SQL expects the word immediately following the single column name in the SELECT clause (of the inner SELECT) to be FROM. The query fails when it finds another column name there instead. The inner SELECT should return a table which contains exactly one column.

The relational model

The relational model was formulated in 1970 by Edgar Codd. His work arose out of a dissatisfaction with the typical DBMSs of the day, in particular with the way in which these systems required both the user and the application to be aware of the internal representation of the data. To use such a system, you had to take account of the precise way in which data was stored, including its sequence, the existence or otherwise of indexes, and the exact access paths to it.

He therefore formulated a theoretical model for an alternative type of DBMS, one that would overcome these problems. This relational model was based on **set theory** ('relation' is a mathematical term for table). Codd and others later developed the theory further. Actual products – first experimental and later commercial – eventually appeared which sought to apply the relational concepts.

In short, a DBMS is relational if:

(a)   To the user, all data is represented as tables and only as tables.

(b)   The result of whatever operations the user can carry out are themselves represented as tables.

The strength of the relational model is its simplicity. An indication of this simplicity is the fact that it is possible to manipulate and search data without any deep technical knowledge of the underlying data structure.

The rules governing the relational model can be considered as falling into three categories:

(a)   Data structure. In terms of normalisation, relations must attain at least the first normal form.

(b)   Integrity. Every table must have a primary key. The column containing the primary key (or the columns containing the various elements which make up the primary key) must be completely filled. Integrity is also governed by rules concerned with foreign keys (see Section 9.3).

(c)   Data manipulation. The model must support **relational algebra**. Relational algebra consists of a set of operations which take, as input, one or two tables, and which yield a new table as output. According to Date (1987, p.363), it is sufficient that the following relational algebra operations are supported: SELECT (selecting rows); PROJECT (selecting columns) and JOIN. SQL's SELECT command caters for all three of these.

The word 'relational' has become something of a marketing term. Vendors use it to describe virtually any DBMS that can work with data from more than one file at the same time. To counter this over-use of the term, Codd formulated a set of firm rules that a DBMS would have to follow in order to be called relational (Date, 1990, p.391 – p.393). In 1990, C.J. Date (p.378) could not identify a single system which supported every aspect of the relational model.

Further reading

Chen, P. (1989), The entity-relationship approach. *Byte*, April, 230–232

Codd, E.F. (1983), A relational model of data for large shared data banks. *Communications of the ACM*, June 1970, **13**, 6, 377–87 (reprinted in: *Communications of the ACM, 25th Anniversary Issue*, January, **26**, 1)

DeMarco, T. (1978), *Structured Analysis and System Specification*, Yourdon Press, New York.

Date, C.J. (1983), *Database, a Primer*, Addison-Wesley, Reading.

Date, C.J. (1987), *A Guide to INGRES*, Addison-Wesley, Reading.

Date, C.J. (1990), *An Introduction to Database Systems. Vol. 1, 5th Edn*, Addison-Wesley, Reading.

Mills, C.W. (1956), *The Power Elite*, Oxford University Press, New York.

Mills, C.W. (1970), *The Sociological Imagination*, New York 1959 (Penguin, Harmondsworth).

Norusis, Marija J. (1988), *SPSS/PC+ v2.0 Base Manual for the IBM PC/XT and PS/2*, SPSS Inc., Chicago.

Pruyt, H. (1991), Relational databases for textual data?, in *Computers in the Humanities and the Social Sciences. Achievements of the 1980s. Prospects for the 1990s. Proceedings of the Cologne Computer Conference 1988* (ed. H. Best, E. Mochmann and M. Thaller), K. G. Saur, München, pp.418–22.

Schipper, D. (1991), A plea for incorporating a textual datamodel in relational databases, in *Computers in the Humanities and the Social Sciences. Achievements of the 1980s. Prospects for the 1990s. Proceedings of the Cologne Computer Conference 1988* (ed. H. Best, E. Mochmann and M. Thaller), K. G. Saur, München, pp.423–6.

Index